The Violence of Men

Cloé Madanes
with James P. Keim and Dinah Smelser

· ·

The Violence of Men

New Techniques for
Working with Abusive Families:
A Therapy of Social Action

Jossey-Bass Publishers
San Francisco

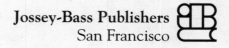

Substantial discounts on bulk quantities of Jossey-Bass books are available to corporations, professional associations, and other organizations. For details and discount information, contact the special sales department at Jossey-Bass Inc., Publishers. (415) 433–1740; Fax (800) 605–2665.

For sales outside the United States, please contact your local Simon & Schuster International Office.

TCF   Manufactured in the United States of America on Lyons Falls Pathfinder Tradebook. This paper is acid-free and 100 percent totally chlorine-free.

Library of Congress Cataloging-in-Publication Data

Madanes, Cloé.
   The violence of men : new techniques for working with abusive families: a therapy of social action / Cloé Madanes, with James P. Keim and Dinah Smelser.
      p.   cm.
   Includes bibliographical references and index.
   ISBN 0–7879–0117–2 (alk. paper)
   1. Violence—Psychological aspects.   2. Abusive men—Rehabilitation.   3. Social action.   4. Sex offenders.   5. Sexual abuse victims.   6. Victims of family violence.   I. Keim, James P.
II. Smelser, Dinah.   III. Title.
RC569.5.V55M333   1995
616.85'82'0081—dc20   95–12339
                                                                                                          CIP

FIRST EDITION
HB Printing   10 9 8 7 6 5 4 3 2

Contents

For each man kills the thing he loves . . .
Oscar Wilde

The lower levels of hell are reserved for those who in times of moral crisis remain neutral.
Dante Allighieri

Acknowledgments

This book was written with the collaboration of James P. Keim and Dinah Smelser. Keim was the therapist in the case presented in Chapter Four, contributing most of the effort and many of the ideas. He was the therapist in several of the cases of juvenile sex offenders in the project described in Chapter Six. The ideas about negotiating differences in marriage, presented in Chapter Seven, are also his. Smelser was the therapist in the majority of the cases of the juvenile sex offender project presented in Chapter Six. Her contribution to that study has been invaluable.

All three of us want to express our gratitude to Councilman William Hanna of Montgomery County, Maryland, who first conceived of the juvenile sex offender project and who, through his support and help, has kept the project alive for eight years.

I would also like to express my gratitude to Alan Rinzler, my editor, for his patience, encouragement, and sound advice. My special appreciation goes to the staff and trainees at the Family Therapy Institute, who over the years have contributed so much to the development of my thinking about therapy.

Introduction

Psychotherapy is the art of finding the angel of hope in the midst of terror, despair, and madness. There is a story from Greek mythology that explains why God created therapists. It is the story of Pandora as told by Virginia Hamilton.

Pandora was a woman made in heaven. Zeus, the creator, wrapped her in a robe of innocence and gave her a box with a surprise inside. Before she left heaven, Apollo said to her, "Pandora, don't ever open the box!"

But Pandora had one defect. She was curious about everything. She had to look into all she saw.

Pandora was sent to Epimetheus and as soon as she entered his house, he fell in love with her beauty. When she told him that she had been sent by Zeus, he said, "There must be a trick somewhere! What do you carry in that box?" Pandora said she didn't know, so Epimetheus put it on the highest shelf, saying that it must be an awful surprise.

When his brother, Prometheus, came home, he warned Epimetheus that Pandora herself was dangerous, not just the box. But Pandora was good. The only problem was that she had to know what was in the box.

One day when she was alone, she decided she would just bring down the box and shake and listen to it without opening it. She put a small chest on a stool, climbed up, and, stretching as high as she could, slid the box toward her. But as she tried to lift it, the box flew out of her hands. There was a great jumble of noise, roars and screams, howls and cries. For a moment the room was dark.

Then out of the box came awful things. Winged things and crawling things, slithering and creeping things, bringing with them a slime of dark and gray despair. There were plagues of sorrow and pain. There was misery, holding its dripping head. Envy took hold of Pandora and tried to tear her hair out. Poverty slid hungrily across the floor.

Pandora tried to cover the box, but it was too late. All of the awful things were clamoring through the house and on out into the street, the town, the whole world.

There was one little thing left quivering on the floor. It must have been at the very bottom of the box. As Pandora held it, she could see its great heart swell and sink in its chest. "I must go," it said, rising weakly to its crooked feet. "But who are you?" Pandora asked.

The thing smiled a wan smile, unfolding its brightly colored wings. "I am Hope," it said. "If I do not hurry, humans will have so little reason to live." And with one great leap, Hope sprang from the room, from the house, and into the world.

Pandora saw Hope catch up to the ugly things of the world. When Hope was among them, the creatures seemed less sure of themselves.

So it was that hunger and poverty, despair and ugliness came into the world of humans. Epimetheus would have to live forever with Pandora, who had let one disaster after another out to torment life.

"Well, it's not all bad," Pandora thought. "There is always Hope."

· · · · · · ·

God created therapists to be like Hope, destined to pursue all the horrors of the world of humans.

It is my wish that this book will bring such hope to therapists working with violent men. Just as violence is the most serious problem between nations, among ethnic groups, and in the streets of our cities, so it is a serious problem in the family. The abuse of wives by husbands and of children by parents constitutes the most insidious, prevalent, and destructive mental health problem that therapists are called upon to solve today. This book will offer some strategies to help therapists go out in the world, like Hope, to tame the monsters and create a reality that is not so bad.

This book addresses the violence of men that most therapists face frequently in their practices. In the first two chapters, we will look at the premises and basic elements of a therapy of social action. Chapters Three through Seven will present case studies and specific steps for working with problems of child abuse, incest, juvenile sexual crime, and marital violence. Chapter Eight deals with some of the difficulties in collaborating with the court system. In Chapter Nine we will look at how to approach the problem of adults who were abused as children. The Epilogue reviews the guidelines, in the form of aphorisms, for a therapy of social action.

The Violence of Men

A Therapy of Social Action

A basic dilemma in psychology is predetermination versus the power to choose. If we think that the individual can decide his or her own future, then we must believe in the individual's responsibility for her own actions and in the possibility that a person can change. On the other hand, believing that the person is predetermined by forces outside of himself makes it difficult to hold an individual responsible for his own actions and to believe in the possibility of change.

The field of psychotherapy is based on the premise that people can change, yet since the origins of psychology, the prevailing view has been that human beings are predetermined by forces outside of their control. What does predetermined mean, and how did the idea that people are predetermined develop?

Predetermination

Let us consider some object that has been manufactured, for example, a book. The manufacturer who produced the book referred to the concept of what a book is and to a method of production that is part of that concept. The manufacturer not only knew that the book is an object produced in a certain way but also knew what it is used for. Therefore, what makes it possible to produce and define a book precedes its presence. The nature of the physical book is pre-determined.

This technical view of the world in which production precedes any kind of existence has run through most of Occidental religious, philosophical, and psychological thinking. God is conceived of as the Creator, as a superior sort of artisan. When God creates, he knows exactly what He is creating. The idea of the human being in the mind of God is similar to the concept of book in the mind of the manufacturer. God produces a person just as the manufacturer following a definition and a technique makes a book. The individual human is the product of a concept in God's mind.

The belief that there is a predetermined essence that precedes existence has also persisted in the idea that people have a human nature. This human nature is found in men and women who have all the same basic qualities. The essence of man and woman is in this human nature that precedes the existence of an individual person. People are born with it.

Another concept has been that there are basic drives or instincts that predetermine our lives. According to Freud, first the sex drive and then the death instinct were the universal driving forces, and each individual's life was the manifestation of these impulses.

Then came the idea of parents as creators. We are what our parents have made us to be. That is, we are the products of our childhood experiences. Just as humans did not turn out to be quite as God intended (thus the fall from grace), so we do not turn out quite as our parents intended. This is the concept of the human being as an object produced by an ignorant, misguided, or even bad-intentioned artisan. This idea has flourished among those who define themselves as adult children, where each individual is seen as the result of a faulty production process and justified as exempt from responsibility.

The concept of the person as the product of chemistry and genetics is another example of the human being as a predetermined object. Both parents and God have been replaced by the physician as manufacturer who produces thought processes and changes moods by chemical means. A person is the product of his or her own chemistry or of what the physician makes of that chemistry.

With systems thinking came another view of human beings as predetermined objects. The person became the product of a social context, of social forces outside the individual's control. God, instincts, parents, chemistry were replaced by the concept of the organization that determines the existence of each of its members. The family, the school, the workplace were the creators, and each individual was a part of the whole self-regulatory mechanism. Parent and child, CEO and factory worker became equal in that they were only parts of a system larger than themselves.

Many family therapists adhered to this concept, trying to escape from ideas of bad parents or bad chemistry, only to find themselves mired in the concept that no one has responsibility. Consequently, the abusive father is the same as the abused child in that both are part of a system that functions as best it can . . . in this best of all possible worlds.

Self-Determination

The opposite of predetermination is the idea of self-determination. There is no manufacturer, no "God," no inner child. The human being exists before he or she is defined by any concept. The person is what she or he conceives herself or himself to be. The person is a subject that acts, not an object that is acted upon.

Respect for each individual's self-determination is the first principle of a therapy of social action. Central to the approach is the belief that a person is capable of making a plan for his or her own future, that each person is responsible for what she or he is. The essence of what is human is the power to choose, the power of self-determination. No matter what the circumstances, there is always a choice to be made. We cannot escape that choice any more than we can escape the fact that the power to choose is the ultimate power. It cannot be taken away from us. We can be manipulated by our parents or through our chemistry. We can be nothing more than a small link in the factory line, or we can be the victims of political torture, but we still have the power to choose.

I believe there is always the power to choose no matter what the circumstances, without ever denying the importance of the family, of chemistry, and of the social context. There is no question that the most direct, most expeditious way to change a person in therapy is to change their social context, their relationship with significant others. But this doesn't mean that the person is predetermined by the context. We all know that a person can change without a change in the context, that the change in the social context can be the result of the change in the individual. We can change through introspection, through reading, through contact with a teacher or therapist. We have the power to choose.

Thus the first move in a therapy of social action is to make each person responsible for their existence and for their actions. There is no Creator, no human nature, no impulses to blame. Chemistry, the inner child, the way we were raised, the system are not responsible. Responsibility is always personal responsibility. It's a well-known fact that some people who were abused, tortured, and suffered horrible hardship became loving, dedicated members of society, while others, raised by loving, giving parents, became murderers. We are what we make of our circumstances.

Does this mean that there is no difference between the rich and the poor, the oppressor and the oppressed? On the contrary, the oppressor and the rich have more power to choose. They have a broader range of choices than the poor and the oppressed. A therapy of social action cannot be used to justify social injustice. It is an approach where the therapist works to increase the range of choices and the power to choose of each individual person.

Personal Responsibility

It's obvious to everyone that when an individual makes a choice, she is deciding not only for herself but also for her children, her parents, her friends, her social network. All her relationships will be affected by her choice. But the individual is responsible not only for her own individuality and her own social network; she is responsible for all human beings.

When we choose for ourselves, we choose for all others. Every single one of our acts creates an image of human beings as we think they ought to be. When we choose to be something, we are asserting the value of what we choose. Nothing can be good for one of us without being good for all. Each person's responsibility involves all mankind.

For example, if I decide to get married and have children, I am asserting the value of family life not only for myself but for all womankind and mankind. In choosing for myself, I choose for everyone. Many people will argue that when they do something no one else is involved. But the opposite is true. Every person's actions affect others, and every person's actions are a model for how others can act.

We cannot explain things away by reference to a fixed or given human nature. In other words, there is no determinism; every person is free. We have no excuse behind us, no justification before us. Each person is responsible for everything he does.

We cannot justify our acts based on the power of emotion. An overwhelming passion does not lead inevitably to certain acts and is therefore not an excuse. Everyone is responsible for his emotions.

Personal responsibility cannot be avoided by finding in the world some omen by which to orient ourselves. Dreams, images, even religious precepts are open to interpretation, and each person will interpret the omen to suit herself. Whatever a person may be, there is a future to be forged.

In forging this future, dilemmas arise that may be extremely difficult to resolve. For example, a person may have to choose between devoting his life to a just cause or to taking care of a loved one. In making such a choice there are no values to guide us. Values are vague and always too broad for the concrete or specific case that we are considering.

One possibility is to go by our feelings. But how do we determine the value of a feeling? A mock feeling and a true feeling are sometimes indistinguishable. To decide that one loves someone and will remain with them, or to remain with that person pretending that one loves them, are not always that different.

Feelings are formed by the acts one performs. That is, it's not true that first one feels, and then one acts on that feeling. The reverse is most often true: action comes first, and subsequently one feels. So one cannot refer to a feeling in order to act upon it. Faced with the dilemma, it's possible to think that one can go to a teacher or therapist for advice. But in choosing a particular teacher or therapist, one is often choosing a certain school of thought and one already knows, therefore, what kind of advice will be offered. No general ethics can show us what is to be done, and there are no omens to guide us.

A further complication is that relying on our own will to forge our future, we can only count on probabilities that our actions will become possible. One cannot count on the success of any plan, no matter how simple. No one can guarantee that a plane will arrive on schedule or that a car will not be hit by a drunk driver. The realm of probabilities is so broad that it is only worth considering those that are directly relevant to one's plan. Often, relying on other people is exactly like counting on the fact that the plane will arrive on time or the car will not be hit. Given that there is no human nature to depend on, one cannot count on human goodness or on man's responsibility for the good of society.

Action

Does all this mean that one should resign oneself to inaction? Quite the contrary. A basic precept of a therapy of social action is "Nothing ventured, nothing gained."

In fact, there is no reality except in action. Compassion only exists in the compassionate deed; violence only exists in the violent act; love is only present in the loving gesture. The absence of action is an action that in itself defines us. The coldness of the relationship is defined by the absence of the warm gesture; nonviolence is the lack of violent acts; a cold heart is present in the absence of compassionate deeds.

Not to act is to act, so we must constantly face decisions as to what is the right action.

The Therapy

So what is a therapy of social action?

A therapy that does not encourage people to derive rational justification for their acts from something stronger than themselves.

A therapy that encourages each individual to face the fact that they are what they have chosen to be and that they must continue to make choices. The essence of what is human is the power of choice. Each individual must choose, act, even though every time we choose, every time we act, we lose something—we lose other choices, other possible actions.

A therapy opposed to labeling people, to fitting them into categories that give a false sense of security by robbing the individual person of responsibility, freedom, and respect for themselves and for others.

A therapy that promotes the recognition that there are no perfect, harmonious relationships and that we cannot be totally free from conflict. In fact, we are constantly faced with conflicting values that are not reconcilable. We cannot resolve the conflict between liberty and organized efficiency, between perfect knowledge and perfect happiness, between the claims of personal life and the claims of work and the public interest.

A therapy that does not pretend to have solutions to the central problems of human life.

A therapy that encourages the recognition of the paradoxes of life and the sense of humor that comes with this recognition.

A therapy that not only encourages each person to take responsibility for her or his own life, but one where the therapist, herself, takes responsibility for the work of the therapy and for its outcome.

A therapy that is not based on any kind of determinism but on the belief instead that no matter what the circumstances, each individual has a range of choices as to what to make of oneself and of one's circumstances. A person is not the product of biology, emotions, the past, the family, or the social context. All these are influences that each individual can choose or refuse to be affected by. A therapy that respects self-determination in each person.

A therapy that recognizes that self-determination is a heavy burden on the individual. The many dilemmas, the difficult choices to be made can best be tolerated when the person has a goal, a purpose in life that transcends himself. To find meaning in life—whether it be in love, beauty, social action, compassion—makes tolerable the responsibility of self-determination and is at the core of a therapy of social action.

Social Action

How are therapy and social action related? Why is this a therapy of social action?

If I believe that in choosing for myself, I choose for others because everything I do affects many others, and if I believe that every one of my acts creates an image of human beings as I think they ought to be, then the way I choose to do therapy is a model for the way I believe all humankind should act. My therapy affects not only those that are directly involved with it but also many others who are indirectly involved.

Therapy has social consequences that go beyond the therapeutic relationship. If my therapy emphasizes the value of introspection, I am asserting the value of introspection for everyone. If my therapy emphasizes the expression of negative feelings, I am encouraging everyone to express their negativity. If my therapy requires repentance and reparation, I am asserting the value of repentance and reparation for everyone. The responsibility of the therapist goes beyond the therapeutic relationship.

If I believe in personal responsibility and I also believe that the only reality is in action—that not to act is to act—then I must recognize that in my therapy I need to protect human rights and to prevent violence. To avoid action, to remain neutral, is to be on the side of violence and abuse.

If I believe that I need to find a meaning in life that transcends my selfish needs, then I believe in finding a meaning in life for everyone.

· · · · · · ·

These are the premises of a therapy of social action. In the next chapter we will look at the most important elements of the approach.

2

The Elements of
Social Action in Therapy

We have seen how a therapy of social action is based on the premises of self-determination and personal responsibility. What are the other essential elements of the approach?

An Interactional View

The most efficient way of changing a person is to change the social context of the person—the ongoing relationships with significant others. These significant others are usually the family, and it is at the level of family relations where the therapist must intervene. Sometimes, however, the most important interactions are with friends, at school, or at the workplace, so the therapist also intervenes in those relationships.

Directives

The most frequent intervention is the directive. We ask people to do certain things in therapy and, between sessions, outside of the therapy room. Directives can be straightforward or indirect, metaphorical or paradoxical.

Most directives involve introducing a minor change in a small segment of behavior, with the expectation that a small change can have larger consequences. A typical directive is for a couple to go out to dinner together or for a father to play with his son. As a change in a relationship develops, other changes take place, and the therapist gives new directives.

An exception is the problem that is the subject of this book. When dealing with violence and abuse, the therapist must often take responsibility for making major changes in people's lives, such as separating a couple or removing a father from the home.

Human Rights

A therapist is not a neutral observer. We have our own goals, and a major goal is the protection of human rights of the people with whom we work, particularly the children. If we don't protect the children and defend their rights, sometimes against the family, sometimes against the school or the court system, nobody else will defend them.

Ethics

Therapists are being called upon not only to protect the human rights of individuals but also to organize family members to do what is morally and ethically right. Morality has come into therapy. We are beginning to understand that what is ethically correct is also therapeutic.

Nowhere is an ethical approach needed as in the problems of violence and abuse, which have reached crisis proportions in our society. Therapists today cannot avoid treating either the victimizers or the victims. In working with these problems, we need to take a clear position about ethical issues. We are usually called upon to decide on such issues as whether a child was abused, who the offender might be, and what will be the consequences for the offender and for the family. Then we must heal the victim, rehabilitate the offender, and prevent further abuse. To be able to do all this, we must be guided by a strong sense of what is right and wrong.

Spirituality

As I have developed methods to work with problems of violence, I've come to rely more and more on ancient wisdom and on spirituality to solve issues of abuse that are as old as the institution of the family itself.

Incest and violence within the family are the subject of Greek tragedy, of the Bible, and of every ancient religion. I realized that with human beings violence and spirituality are related, so that certain kinds of attacks on a person are attacks on the spirit of that person. So in training therapists to work with problems of violence and sexual abuse, I teach them to address issues of spiritual pain. And I notice how difficult it is for therapists to talk about spirituality.

What is the spirit? It is difficult to define, yet we know it is there. Perhaps it is similar to the idea of beauty. We cannot explain what it is, yet we can recognize it when we see it. Perhaps we are only aware of the spirit when it hurts. People who have suffered from certain forms of violence know that pain. Yet it is so difficult for therapists to recognize this spiritual pain.

All our training as therapists appears to have been designed to deny the existence of anything spiritual. As I pondered the reasons for this denial, I thought about the origin of the field of psychotherapy. We are, in fact, very young, only about 100 years old. Psychotherapy as a field of inquiry probably began with the publication of Freud's early writings. When Freud began to struggle to establish psychotherapy as a profession, he had to be careful to differentiate from the hypocrisy of organized religion in the Victorian era. But in throwing out religion, he threw away the whole concept of spirituality.

Today, 100 years later, we are established as a profession, and there is no longer the risk that we will be confused with religion. So we can bring spirituality back into the realm of therapy and accept that we are called on to heal not only the mind but also the spirit, and that without healing the spirit we cannot live in harmony with one another.

The Family as Self-Help Group

A shift has taken place in our culture over the last fifteen years, from institutional help to self-help. For decades we were dependent on the protection of institutions such as the government, the medical establishment, the corporation, and the school system. But in the last twenty years it has become apparent that we've lost the war on poverty, education has declined, and we have learned to mistrust medicine with its unnecessary interventions.

Self-help began to replace these institutions and has become a part of American life. Community groups are acting across the nation to prevent crime, to feed the elderly, to build houses, to promote health, and to educate children.

Family therapy originated in the 1950s as part of the development from the individual to the system as the unit for study. It was difficult to make the transition from focusing on the individual to focusing on the relationship between individuals. As therapists struggled to change their point of view, some concepts from an individual approach were inappropriately transferred to the systems approach. Family therapy was thought to be a "cure" for the whole family that was supposed to be "sick" or "pathological." In fact, family members can be loving or hostile, hopeful or pessimistic, tolerant or intolerant, but there is no such thing as a sick or healthy family.

The family is the ultimate self-help group. Families are invited to therapy to help the therapist solve the problems of the individuals who consult them. There is no one that can help or interfere as much with the well-being of a person as those who have ongoing relationships, who have a history, a present, and a future together.

Reorganizing the Tribe

As the ultimate self-help group, the family is the unit of society for tolerance, compassion, and love. The therapist changes relationships by reorganizing the natural network of the family, the tribe, and then disengaging, leaving family members to care for and protect one another.

The idea that the family is a self-help group became more apparent to me as I began to work with more and more cases of abuse, neglect, and incest where the very existence of the family unit was threatened. I had to find protectors—strong, responsible people in the extended family or in the community—and transfer responsibility to them.

For example, if an adolescent had been abused by a father, a responsible uncle or grandmother could be put in charge of supervising the family to make sure that this would not happen again. If a child had to be removed from the home, she could be placed with relatives rather than with strangers. In working with these problems, I realized that I was relying on the family as a self-help group where children can help their parents, or uncles and aunts can take charge, or grandparents can be responsible, or occasionally everyone can help one another.

Therapists need to reunite family members when they have become estranged from one another, especially when parents try to expel their children literally or emotionally. In these cases, before doing anything else in therapy, one has to arrange for the family to contain the children without expulsion. It's important to understand that in the parents' mind, expulsion may not be contradictory with wanting to love and protect their children. Parents with low self-esteem may love their children and, precisely because they love them, want to give them away to others, that is, to people who they think will be better parents. The therapist needs to organize the extended family to bolster the parents' self-esteem so that they can contain their children. This is one of the many ways in which the family network is helpful.

The Family Network as Unit for Therapy

What is a family network? For centuries, the pyramid structure was the way we organized ourselves. From the Catholic Church to the army, General Motors and the Department of Social Services, power flowed from the pyramid's top, down to its base; from the pope, the general, the CEO, down through the lieutenants and managers, to the workers and soldiers at the bottom.

But in the sixties and seventies, we began to demystify hierarchies. The United States' economy, based on hierarchical structures, fell into trouble. Rising in its place was the new information economy where greater flexibility was necessary and hierarchies were inappropriate.

The belief in the efficacy of hierarchies began to crumble, and the new networking model evolved. A network is the process that links clusters of people. It is a powerful tool for social action. This is the way the women's movement began, as well as the consumer organizations, rehabilitation networks, food networks, environmental protection networks, education and information networks, and many others. Networks offer the horizontal link, the egalitarian relationship that those who take seriously the ideology of democracy so crave. Hierarchies are about power and control. Networks are about empowering and nurturing.

Changes developed in the work of therapists coinciding with these changes in the culture. There was a transition from thinking in hierarchies to thinking in networks. Therapists began to notice that seemingly powerful and competent adults can be helpless and incompetent parents. Even more interesting, we realized how little children, apparently helpless, can be powerful helpers in the family.

The family appears to be a traditional hierarchical organization with parents in charge of the children. But perhaps, in fact, a family is rarely organized in this way. How often does a parent side with a child to help the other parent? How many children help their parents' marriage stay together? How many children succeed in separating their parents? These questions and many similar questions led therapists to think that perhaps to organize a family in a hierarchical model was not necessarily the best idea.

Approaches to therapy were developed that violate the model of the traditional family hierarchy and are based instead on a new model of the family as a network. The communication style in this new model is lateral, diagonal, and bottom-up. A network is like a fishnet where the nodes are all linked together in a three-dimensional structure.

A family can be a complicated organization. There are parents and children, stepparents and stepchildren, grandparents, uncles, aunts, cousins, second cousins, brothers and sisters, stepgrandparents, stepuncles and stepaunts, friends of the family, neighbors, and members of the community. A therapist needs to think in terms of self-help within this network: who can initiate change and who can help whom. There are the obvious hierarchical possibilities: parents help children; grandparents help parents and children. There are also lateral possibilities: parents help each other, children help each other, the older generation helps each other, or the younger generation helps each other. There are also bottom-up choices: children can help parents; parents can help grandparents; the younger generation can help the older generation.

The therapist looks to enter the network through whoever is the best resource for initiating a positive change in the family. In many situations that we face today, when parents are drug addicted, abusive, neglectful, or ill, a lateral or bottom-up approach is more conducive to change than a hierarchical one.

Typically, the sequence in therapy is as follows. If a therapist is not making progress with an individual or a family in therapy, the therapist expands the unit. Siblings, grandparents, uncles and aunts, cousins and relatives, and, ultimately, members of the community are brought in. Eventually a level is reached where change takes place, because every time new people are approached there are new points of view and different resources. Arranging for these new influences enriches everyone's life.

Violence Is the Problem

All the problems that come to therapy today can be subsumed under the category of the violence that people inflict on one another. This violence may be overt as in physical punishment or sexual assault, or it may be covert as in neglect or emotional abuse. It can be inflicted on others or on oneself.

This book offers strategies for solving the covert as well as the overt violence of men. The strategies may apply equally well to violent women, but I haven't had as much experience with violent women as I have with violent men. The focus will be on the types of men's violence that usually come to a therapist's office: child abuse, wife abuse, and sexual molestation. The book doesn't deal with murder, ritualistic abuse by cults, serial killers, or torturers, although I assume that the techniques I've developed may also prevent men from engaging in some of these more serious crimes.

· · · · · · ·

In the next chapter we will look at a therapy of social action in a family where the father was physically violent with his daughters.

3

The Caged Animal

A family came to therapy because Kristen was a misbehaving, rebellious seventeen-year-old daughter. The therapist organized the parents to clarify rules and consequences if the rules were disobeyed, and the girl's behavior improved.

But the therapist also noticed that the parents were always angry at each other despite several unsuccessful attempts to improve their relationship. The parents were in their early forties, the father was a prominent scientist, and the mother took care of the home and the children (three girls ranging in age from twelve to seventeen). The parents hardly spoke with each other and had not had sexual relations in two years. They did not want to separate, and they did not want to improve their relationship.

Kristen's behavior improved after a few months, and, even though the therapist was concerned about the couple, the therapy was interrupted. A few months later the parents called to say that Kristen had made a suicide attempt with an overdose of pills and was in the hospital. The precipitating event had been that while driving her to school in his car, the father threw a cup of hot coffee in her face, angry at something she had said. Apparently this was not the first time that he had been violent with his daughter.

The therapist met with the family and was shocked to find that there had been many episodes of violence. Concerned because he had not realized before that the father was violent, the therapist referred the family to me, thinking that it was best to have a fresh start after the crisis.

Goals

For my first session with the family, I planned to find out exactly how many and what kind of incidents of violence the father had engaged in. I was not discarding the possibility of sexual abuse and planned to be sensitive to any indications in this regard. I would see the whole family together, the girls separately, Kristen by herself, and then the family together again. The purpose of breaking up the family into these subgroups was to elicit all the information about violence, since it's often easier for children to talk when they are not in the parents' presence.

I also wanted, in this session, for the father to recognize that he had sole responsibility for his violence. No one else was to blame. He had to state, in front of the family, that violence is wrong and that no provocation justifies hitting a daughter.

In a therapy of social action each person is responsible for their actions. No matter what the provocation, there is always a choice to be made. The father elected to behave violently. There were many other possible behaviors open to him, and he chose to be violent against his daughter. His nature, his character, or the power of his emotions are no justification for violence. I would ask him to apologize, not only to Kristen but to each of the children whom he had hurt. A violent father not only has to believe that he has sole responsibility for his violence and that his violence is wrong; he also has to express this belief to those he has hurt and convey his sorrow for his violent actions.

When meeting with Kristen alone, I would explore the possibility of another suicide attempt in order to make sure that it wouldn't happen. I would explore her interests and encourage her to have a dream, something to look forward to, that I could help her accomplish, to ensure that she would want to stay alive. I would ask her to promise me and the family that she would not hurt herself again.

The First Session

I met with the whole family, and with gentle but direct questioning of every family member quickly brought out all the different incidents of violence. The father had hit Kristen several times in the last two years. Once he punched her so hard that she had passed out on the kitchen floor. He had punched the second daughter in the stomach on two occasions but had never hit the youngest. I carefully went around the circle getting everyone's agreement that these events had actually happened.

Then I turned to the father. "Do you feel it's wrong what you do?"

"Obviously," he said, stroking his beard nervously.

"Why? Why is it wrong?"

"Well," he said, "I think it's a violation of somebody's privacy in a physical sense. It's absurd. It's not something that I'm proud of myself for, the things that I've done. Yet, I've done them, and I would like that not to happen again."

"It's more than absurd," I said. "It's very painful because it comes from the father, right? The person who should protect and love, not hurt. This isn't like an occasional spanking of a young child—this is an impulsive hitting."

"That's right," he said.

"I'm going to ask you to do something a little difficult. I would like you to come close to each of the ones that you've hurt, starting with Kristen, and ask her . . . tell her that you're sorry. I was going to say, 'Ask her to forgive you,' but I don't think that you should ask for forgiveness. She can forgive you eventually if she wants to, but right now you should just tell her how sorry you are. I understand that she provokes you. I'm sure of that. Yet your response should never be violence because you're the adult in the situation. Would you do this?"

"Sure." The father knelt on the floor next to Kristen. He whispered, "I'm sorry, I'm very sorry."

Then, tearful, he knelt next to the second daughter, Caroline: "I'm sorry."

The mother was silently crying. He sat back on his chair.

"Was that sincere?" I asked the girls.

Kristen shook her long blond hair "No" as she spoke quickly and with the characteristic adolescent irritability. "I have a problem with his saying 'I'm sorry,' because I can't really identify with it. I feel that if I had done something, I had a reason to do it and I'm never going to feel sorry for anything I did. But I guess this is just kind of my idea. I mean, someone can feel sorry, but I can't really understand it."

"So you grew up never hearing 'I'm sorry'?" I asked.

"Well, I'm sure I have but I just, I don't think. . . ."

"Because things are repeated anyhow?" I interrupted.

"Yeah, things are repeated anyhow, and I think that if you've done something, you've done it. Don't take it back. And you did it for a reason, whether the reason was right or wrong or whether it was a real reason or an imaginary reason, you did it."

I realized that Kristen was desperately trying to find an excuse for her father, to protect him in some way. I turned to Caroline. "Do you think he was sincere?"

"I guess so."

To the wife: "You think he was sincere?"

"I guess," she was sitting stiffly now, with her white blouse buttoned all the way up to her neck.

"He was?" I insisted.

"Yes, I think that he's sincere."

I had almost been moved to tears myself by the father's apology, his tears, and his sadness. Yet no one in the family seemed to have much compassion for him. I turned to the father. "See, this is one of the consequences of your violence—it hardens them. It hardens them a lot. And you don't want them to grow up to be so harsh with other people."

I turned to the mother and the daughters. "You're tough, and it's alright to be tough . . . but sometimes. . . ."

I found out from the mother that immediately after taking the overdose of pills, Kristen had come to her and told her. Kristen said she didn't want to die and didn't know why she had done this. I understood that Kristen's behavior was a cry for help. The father's violence had to stop. She promised the family and me that she wouldn't hurt herself again.

In talking with Kristen alone, I discovered that her hopes were typical of adolescence. She wanted more independence. Yet she talked about how she longed for less tension in the home. She had doubts about going off to college, even though she had been admitted to the school of her choice. This reluctance to leave home is typical of young people whose parents are in a miserable relationship. If Kristen stayed home, the parents' anger could be focused on her rather than on each other. So I knew that for Kristen to continue to develop normally, I had to improve the parents' marriage.

I ended the session arranging to see the parents alone next time, without the girls. I wanted to bring out all the truth about the violence. I wasn't satisfied yet that I knew about each episode. I invited the previous therapist, Richard, to join us in the next session.

Goals for the Second Session

My goals for this session were:

1. To find out about all the episodes of violence.
2. To make sure that the father took responsibility for his actions.
3. To explore the link between the father's violence toward Kristen and his marital problems with Laura. If there were such a link, then it would be appropriate for me to work on marital issues at the same time that I worked on family issues. I had to be careful about how I approached the marriage, because with the previous therapist, the parents had refused to focus on the marriage.

4. To prevent the parents from minimizing the seriousness of the father's violence.

5. To begin to change the meaning that violent behavior had for the father, so that instead of expressing power, it represented impotence.

    In every therapy for a problem of violence, the therapist has to focus on the metaphor, the hidden meaning of what the violence represents to the violent person. Usually violence, for the violent man, means manliness, power, control, force, and self-determination. The therapist has to change the metaphor, so that violence comes to mean impotence, helplessness, immaturity, and defeat. The way this meaning can be attributed depends on the situation of each particular person, on the history, fears, desires, and frustrations of each violent man.

6. To find out about violence in previous generations, particularly in the mother's family, since she was the one that most seemed to minimize the importance of the father's violence. Discussing the consequences of violence in previous generations motivates people to prevent it from continuing in the present.

7. To encourage the father to report himself to Protective Services. In this way, rather than if I reported him, he would be taking full responsibility for his actions.

The Session

The mother started by saying, "Ken [the father] constantly tells me that he doesn't like me and has been talking about leaving the family."

Ken interrupted her, saying, "At this point I don't feel that I'm contributing anything that's positive to the family."

"You mean that if you continue in this situation at home, you can only be negative, and it's better not to be there?" I asked.

"Right."

I realized that Ken was threatening leaving the family as an attempt to regain the power he was losing. Perhaps he thought that if he threatened the mother with a separation, she and the girls would back off and stop addressing his violence, and I would back off in the therapy from focusing on him. It's typical of violent men that, when confronted with their violence, they will escalate and either threaten with more violence, even against the therapist, or threaten abandoning the family. I had to call his bluff and not let him silence me or his wife, as he had done in the past when during months of therapy no one had brought up his violence.

"And there's a point to that, because it's a very dangerous situation," I said, referring to the idea that perhaps he should leave the family.

"But I see it as dangerous if he's not there," said the wife.

"How?" I asked.

"For Kristen," she answered tearfully. "She blames herself so much. Her attitude is 'When I'm out of the house, things will be better.' She thinks that she is 90 percent of why the family doesn't get along and that when she's not there, the family will be better."

"Because she's such a source of irritation?"

"Uh-huh, and she's so volatile."

"So she doesn't know how much is her responsibility and how much is her father's responsibility," I said. "She's confused about that."

"Right," said the mother.

"So one of the issues, not only for you, Ken, but also for Kristen, is not knowing whether you're going to leave or stay, live or die. Kristen's problem about not knowing whether she wants to live or die seems similar to your problem not knowing whether you want to stay in the home or not. And I think that it's part of the confusion about who is whom and who does what to whom, which is very important to clarify. And the issue of responsibility is also very important to clarify, for the sake of both of you, and of Kristen, and of the other two girls." I took the conversation back to the issue of the father's responsibility for his own violence, which was the real issue here, not his threat of leaving the family.

"I agree that the issue of responsibility is something that's very muddy," said Ken. "I don't understand the connection between Kristen wanting to die, and I truly don't believe that she wants to die, and whether I want to leave."

"Well, you've been talking about it," I said. "I don't know whether you want to leave or not. All I know is that you said, 'I'm going to leave,' and then you didn't."

"Right," agreed Ken.

"Kristen says 'I'm going to kill myself,' and then she doesn't."

"Right. OK. Similar in that way."

"And I think it's very important for all of us, and also for the girls who are not here today, to clarify exactly what the truth is, what has happened, what are the family secrets. Who did what to whom. And then to have a fresh start. I don't believe in holding people together when they're not happy together. But I believe that if you're living in a situation that leads to violence, it's not a good situation."

"Right," said Ken.

"So I'm not going to try to keep you in that situation."

I turned to Laura, the mother, who was tearful. "I sympathize with you in that I know it's hard to think of a separation when you love someone, but I also think you're caught in a very difficult situation. You don't want a man to be with you who constantly tells you that he doesn't like you."

Laura began to explain some of the details of Ken's violence. "When Kristen and he used to get into it, she would call him a bastard, and he would spank her. Looking back now, it was out of hand. At the time, I had backed out; I was trying to let them have their own relationship. I was trying to stay out of being in the middle of it, because I was in too far. But it's not a constant kind of thing. I wouldn't think of it as a violent home."

"I would," I said.

In the first session, while discussing the father's violence with the girls and with the parents, I had also carefully explored the possibility of sexual abuse and was certain that there hadn't been any. Yet the intensity of the violence in the father-daughter relationship had connotations of sexual abuse. Violent physical contact can have the characteristics of a sexual perversion even when it does not involve any contact with sexual organs.

The mother answered my statement with shock. "You would?"

"Yes, and I think that it's pretty bad. I think it's very important to clarify. . . ."

She interrupted me, "I don't see that."

". . . exactly what happened," I continued.

Laura began to explain one of the episodes of violence. "Kristen was in the kitchen, and Ken said, 'I've hurt your daughter. Go to her.' And I said, 'If you've hurt her, you go to her.' And he left the house. I went in the kitchen and she was on the floor. I asked her if she was OK, and she said, 'I don't know, I don't know if I passed out or not.' And she was very upset, but my interpretation at the time was that she had been awfully dramatic."

Richard, the previous therapist, who was sitting with us in this session, was shocked at the mother's denial. "You can't possibly have amnesia for the things you said two weeks ago, sitting exactly where I'm sitting," said Richard.

"And what was that?" asked the mother as if she didn't know what he was talking about.

"We were talking about the violent episode, and you said that you felt terrible because over the years these things had happened, and you were acknowledging them and recognizing that they were continuing to go on. And you sat here in this very spot."

"I'm acknowledging it . . . ," she sobbed and broke down crying.

"Are you worried that if you talk about this he's going to leave home?" I asked.

"Well, I feel that he's like a caged animal."

"Are you worried that he's going to hurt you, or are you worried that he's going to leave?"

"I'm not worried that he'll hurt me," she answered.

"Are you worried that he'll hurt the girls?" I asked.

"I'm worried about his temper. I see him lose control, and I'm always afraid of it. There's always a tension in the house, and I always worry that he might get upset." Laura cried as she talked.

"And why is he a caged animal?" I asked.

"I guess I see him really trying. I see him trying in my mind. You won't agree with this," she answered. "In my mind I see him trying very, very hard but it's always, 'If the house were straightened out, or there was less of this or that mess, or you paid less attention to the children. . . .' There's always something he focuses on, but he really works on whatever he's focusing on. I mean, he's a very single-minded person. And I've never seen him work on what I think needs to happen, but I guess it's a hope that he will work on that some day."

I was thinking about how, like every abusive parent, the father was extremely immature and needy. "Still, that doesn't answer how he's an animal," I said.

"I'm sorry, I got off the track. It's like now he knows that it has to change. He feels terrible about what's happened, but he doesn't see a way out. He knows it has to change, he wants it to change, but here he is—he's stuck in the cage and he's grasping for a way to. . . ." She was looking for the right word.

"And the way to help him," I said, "is not to deny, not to cover up, not to distort, and to help your husband face up to the responsibility of whatever happened, and to help him do the reparation that has to be done. . . ."

"You see what I have trouble with . . . ," said Laura.

I continued, "Because if not, you're treating him like he is an animal."

Laura cried, "No! But I guess I'm having trouble saying that it's a violent family! I guess it's not. . . ."

"I don't believe in a violent family," I said. "Individuals are violent. What do you mean 'a violent family'?"

"No, but. . . ."

"I don't believe that your three daughters are violent. Maybe they are, but I haven't seen that."

"No," said Laura, "they're not. It's violence, and I don't know how to. . . ."

Ken interrupted, "Yes, yes, there has been violence over the past five years, and I think we've discussed each of the episodes probably several times. And in each case it's been my fault. There's no question about that. I don't have any question about it. I don't think anyone else does either. But I think what Laura is trying to say is that as bad as that is, even worse is the level of tension that we all feel when we're in our home, independent of the fear of violence on anybody's part. I think, . . . is that what you're trying to say, Laura?"

She nodded agreement.

"Is this an accurate description," I asked Ken, "what your wife described, that your well-being is so dependent on what the rest of the family is doing or how they behave toward you, so that, for example, if the house were more straightened out, then you'd be happier? Is this an accurate description?" I was beginning the process of redefining the meaning of the father's violence. I redefined his demands and his bad temper, changing them from the self-righteous assertiveness that he probably experienced to a dependence on his wife and family. Instead of a powerful man, he was like a dependent child: his happiness and well-being depended on whether the house was straightened out.

"I have to break that, the answer to that question, up into time frames. Yes, there was a time in which I thought that was the case." Ken was trying to be very rational.

"Let me go back to one thing that I thought was important," I said. "You said that you thought that it was all your responsibility." Once again I took him back to his responsibility for the violence.

"What was?" asked Ken.

"The violence."

"Yes," he said.

"The episodes of violence were your responsibility," I said.

"No question about it," he answered.

"It's very important to clarify that with the girls," I said. "And it's very important to have in the open what were the episodes, exactly what happened, and how it was your responsibility. Because this secrecy does a lot of psychological harm. The fear that the child has that somehow it was her fault. . . ."

The mother interjected tearfully, "That's the part that worries me."

"That all the unhappiness is her fault," I continued. "And I don't think you appreciate your wife thinking of you as a caged animal. She describes you as someone . . . like a caged, frightened animal . . . whom a little girl can come into a room and take advantage of."

The mother's metaphor of a caged animal had been of a powerful, frightening creature. I deliberately changed the metaphor to that of an impotent, scared, and immature being. I had to take any symbol of power or masculinity out of the image of a violent man. He wasn't powerful and threatening; instead, he was imprisoned, frightened, and easily tormented. When working with violent men, it's crucial to change the metaphor of violence from power and virility to impotence and ridicule.

"Why would you live with that kind of a description of yourself?" I added.

"Also," said Ken sadly, "I haven't been able to show affection."

"The reason for that," I said, "is that when certain very bad things happen in a family, it's impossible to correct anything unless there is some recognition of what happened, some acceptance, some agreement about what happened. And an apology for what happened. So for her to receive your affection or for you to try to give it before that happens—it just can't be."

"I'm having such a hard time with this," said the mother. She was still crying.

I turned to her. "What were the worst things that have happened to you in your life?" I suspected that Laura was so tearful, and that it was so difficult for her to acknowledge the reality of her husband's violence, because there had been violence in her childhood.

"What do you mean in my life?"

"In your whole life, not necessarily in your married life."

"Well, you see," she said, "the part that I'm having a whole lot of trouble with is whether or not. . . . I'm really confused!"

"Did you have a very bad childhood?" I asked.

"I grew up in a violent home, very violent home. So maybe by comparison, this isn't violent. It's not even in the same category."

"Were you abused?"

"No."

"Who was?"

"My mother."

"How was she abused?"

She sighed. "Now my father is a recovering alcoholic. But from when I was ten on, he was violent. And the trick in the family was that anything that we did wrong—like two of us fought or the car didn't start—anything we did wrong, he never yelled at us—he took it out on my mother. If we made any mistake at all or he found out about anything, she'd get it. And he was very violent. . . ."

"So that you always felt responsible." I encouraged her to go on.

"We were always responsible for her and responsible for each other. We had a system—there were seven of us—of covering up. An unbelievable system of covering for each other and making sure that he didn't know. It was also a family secret. Nobody else knew. . . ."

"Perhaps he wouldn't have been able to hit her if others had known, right?" I asked her.

"Right. Well, it was horrible. I have a brother who lived with a machete under his bed, you know. It was a very violent home. But. . . ."

"Did he abuse your siblings?"

"He would get after my brothers."

"Who was the person that loved you most in your life?"

"I don't know how to answer that. Ken has loved me very much. As violent as my father was, he adored me. My mother, I'm very, very close to my mother. All my brothers are very close friends."

"So you know that there can be terrible tension and violence and still be love," I said.

"Yes, and it was very clear at home. I knew my father loved me dearly, and yet there was terrible violence."

"So perhaps you're more tolerant than most people to that kind of conflict. You could live in a bad situation like that forever because you always have," I said.

"Hm-mm."

I turned to Ken. "What was the worst situation, the worst thing that happened to you?"

"I think what I'm going through now is the worst thing that's ever happened," he answered.

"What part of it?"

"The realization of some of the things I've done . . . is probably the most devastating, the most uncomfortable part, the most . . . yet the worst part I think is the frustration that I feel on two different levels. One is the difficulty in communicating with Laura, and the other is the frustration of not being able to do anything positive about what I know is a bad situation. The fact that I hurt my children. The fact that yesterday I told the children I was leaving. These are things that I had hoped would never happen." He was sobbing as he spoke. "And I didn't have any control over them happening."

"Last time you were here," I said, "you apologized to the girls and that was a very good beginning. I would like you to remember each episode with the girls and acknowledge your responsibility, that they did not provoke it, that whatever misbehavior, the punishment is not justified, and to apologize to them again. Particularly to Kristen, but it's very important for all three of them to have a sense of reality, so that everyone is in agreement about what actually happened and why it was bad, why it was wrong. That is a first step that is very important. And of course it's very important for this not to happen again."

"That's exactly right," he said.

I was thinking that in Laura's family, her mother had paid for what Laura did wrong. In Kristen's family, I suspected that Kristen paid for what Laura did wrong.

I asked Ken, "Now to what extent when you hit Kristen are you really wanting to hit Laura?"

"To a considerable extent. I don't know how to put percentages on this, but certainly the last episode in the car was mostly directed against Laura. I didn't realize this until afterward. . . ."

"And why don't you hit Laura directly instead?" I asked, realizing to what extent Kristen was offering herself in sacrifice to protect her mother. The father's frustration probably stemmed mostly from the lack of affection and the total absence of sex with Laura. My guess was that when Kristen felt the father's anger against her mother mounting, she would provoke him to take out his frustration by hitting her and so spare her mother. Curiously, Laura had managed to be involved with a violent father and a violent husband, yet she was always spared from the violence itself.

Ken answered my question: "I wouldn't think about hitting Laura . . . I can't. . . ."

"Are you afraid of her?"

"In some ways, sure. What leads to the violence is frustration." He turned to Laura. "I guess one time that you ended up on the floor, I was puzzled about how it happened but I confessed it was my fault. I didn't hit her but I pushed her," he clarified for me. "I did something physical to get her out of the way. At that time I realized that I couldn't possibly do that and be protective." He sighed deeply. "I kept doing things that were turning her off. When I felt the frustration level going up, I would just turn the switch off. I would leave the house. So I had developed protective mechanisms. And I guess with Kristen in the car, those protective mechanisms weren't in place."

"It's still important," I said, "to go back in time and remember every bad thing that happened between you. I realize that it's very difficult for you, Laura, since your vision about what is bad is really horrible, because of your childhood. So it's difficult for you to be realistic. But it doesn't protect your daughters when you take this attitude. You've got to realize that you were in a situation where your behavior could result in terrible punishment to your mother, and Kristen is in a situation where her behavior results in protectiveness toward you. She gets hit instead of you, and you don't want that."

"I saw that clearly," said Laura tearfully, "the day she took it away from Caroline and took it on herself." (She was referring to an episode described in the previous session where Kristen had managed to get hit instead of Caroline, whom the father was about to attack.)

"Let me make some suggestions, and I'll put them in writing if you want," I said. "I would like for you, Ken, to minimize the time that you spend with the girls, to minimize the time that you spend at home. This is not forever, just the next few weeks. Instead, you must concentrate on an adult life with your wife.

"For the next few weeks, be the kind of father who comes home in the evening, says hello to the girls, then goes to his study and waits until his wife is free to join him. You can talk to the girls just enough to find out that they're alright, ask about their homework, and that's it. On the weekend, I would like you to do whatever you're interested in doing but make sure you do it with your wife. So go out to a movie, go out to dinner, go out with friends, or whatever.

"I would like you, Laura, not to enlist his help for carpooling or for anything. The children and the house are your domain, your work, and you have to figure out how to arrange it. You both have said that the worst thing that has happened to you in your life is the conflict between you, so you've got to get those three girls out of that conflict so that you can meet each other again and resolve it. You're confused about who works where and who's in charge of what in relation to the girls. So the girls keep coming into the relationship trying to save you, but they just make things worse. I don't want Ken to be replacing you in your motherly duties. I don't want him to be that kind of a father at the moment. The first thing one has to do when there's too much tension and violence is separate from the situation so that it cannot happen."

I was thinking that the first thing to do in situations of violence is to separate victim and victimizer. I continued, "I want you to have conversations about adult things, about the two of you, and have only a small percentage of the time devoted to the girls.

"For a while," said Laura, "we were going to try to go out on weekends. . . ."

I looked at Ken. "I think that's what gives you the feeling of being caged. Aside from your work, you don't have an adult life. You come home, and it's never perfect, never the way it should be because it can't be satisfying to you; it's too much time spent that way. I think if you have more of an adult lifestyle, issues of violence will stop. You'll be able to meet each other and find each other again. I can't guarantee you'll like each other, but at least you'll have the opportunity. And I think you probably will like each other, since maybe that's why both of you are saying that the worst thing in life is the conflict between you." I turned to Ken. "You're on vacation from the girls for a while. Does that make sense to you?"

"Yes," he said emphatically.

"So you will protect this relationship"—I made a gesture encompassing him and his wife—"from intrusions from other people. Can I have a set day and time when you're going to meet and talk about the girls and at no other time?" I knew that Laura had been avoiding Ken sexually and emotionally, yet she had been very upset at the idea that he might leave the family. I thought that she hung on to him by pretending that his help with the girls was essential, when in fact she was very competent to take care of their needs. The children were what held the couple together, and I had to limit their power. So I began by suggesting that they talk about the girls only once a week.

"Sunday evenings," said Laura.

"Where? It would be better out of the house."

"We'll go for a walk."

"I don't like a walk," I said. "Excuse me, but it can be ended abruptly. I think it's better to sit in a restaurant where you have to order a meal and eat, so you're stuck there for half an hour at least."

"I see one big problem with this," said Laura, "and that is communication. When Kristen is expressing the kinds of things she's expressing. . . ."

"Don't you want to talk to each other?" I asked.

"But then all the responsibility is on my shoulders," said Laura, crying again.

"Why?"

Ken helped me out: "She'd like to know that if she needs help, that I'm there and willing to come help and support her."

"That's exactly what I don't want to happen," I said. "That does not work."

"I think I feel pretty unsure myself," said Laura, "when Kristen is expressing some of the things she's expressing."

"Call us," I said, referring to myself and Richard, the previous therapist. "Also, if it gets too much for you, call your mother and tell her everything." I turned to Ken. "You made a big step forward today and last time in accepting your responsibility and resolving what you've done in terms of the violence with the girls. Now there's one more thing that you need to do. Call or write Protective Services and tell them what's happened. I would like the two of you to do that jointly."

"Protective Services is . . . ah . . . ," said Ken.

"The Department of Social Services," I said, "in the town where you live. Explain to them that this is what's happened in the family, that you have been violent toward Kristen on whatever occasions, and toward Caroline, that you are in therapy, that you are controlling yourself, and this is not going to happen again. In your conscience you will feel better after doing this. It's very important. So will your wife because she will not be helping you to cover it up."

"OK," said Ken.

"She values so much being a good mother," I continued. "You value so much that in her. And this is being a good mother; covering up is not."

"And the girls should read this letter?" asked Ken.

"Yes," I said. "Get a copy of the letter for the girls to read, and I'd prefer for that to happen in the session here."

"Alright," said Ken.

"Ask your wife if she's willing to help you," I said.

"In the writing of this?" he asked.

"Yes."

"Will you help?" he asked Laura.

"I'm having a really hard time," she said. Then she began to cry. We waited in silence for her to control herself. "I don't know," she went on, "I'm having a real hard time. I guess I can't even . . . I have trouble even accepting it."

"I know," I said, "but that's part of the problem."

"Accepting what?" asked Ken.

"Accepting that this happened," I answered.

Laura was crying. "It's not like I'm trying to cover up . . . and that's why I was getting really mad at you."

"I know, I know," I said.

"Because you kept saying these things. . . . I wanted to say 'No, you don't understand.'"

"I know," I said, "but what makes it possible for violence to happen is the secrecy. When things are out in the open, then violent behavior cannot happen because society can protect us from that.

A big step forward is coming to see us. A big step forward is talking about it, meeting all together as a family. Make it public and it won't happen again."

"But what does that do to the kids?" asked Laura.

"It confirms their reality, because what makes a person crazy is to know that something truly happened and to be told that it didn't."

"I know," said Laura.

"Children can cope with many difficult situations in life. I think that you can say to your children, 'I'm not as adult as I would like to be; I'm not the perfect person that I would like to be; far from that—I lose control; I do bad things.' They can understand that; they can cope with that. What is very difficult to cope with is the incongruity of the situation, the lying—that is very difficult to cope with."

"Some things are making sense," said Laura. "I remember when I was a child I went to a priest and told him that I thought my father had attacked my mother with a knife. And he looked at me and he said, 'You're crazy—don't ever speak like that again.' So I spent the next year thinking I must be crazy. She said she did it on a can opener, and I tried for hours to cut my arm on a can opener the way hers was cut! But I know what you're saying: we did keep it a total secret. We didn't talk among each other."

"That's right," I said, "and that's how it continued and continued." I felt very tired. The effort to help Laura to have this insight had drained me.

"Jesus!" said Laura.

"OK, so we have an agreement?" I asked.

"I'm having a hard time with that," said Laura. She was still crying.

"You will be so relieved," I said. "It will be so much better after it's done. And you don't have to do this in an intellectual way; you don't have to put labels on what happened." Laura was crying loudly. "Just describe the facts," I continued. "It's the right thing to do by your husband and by the girls, and also for yourself." Laura blew her nose loudly. I looked at the husband. "You're going to help her to be strong and do this?"

He nodded agreement.

"Alright. Next time you'll bring us a copy of that letter, and you'll come with the girls."

I knew that I should report the father to Protective Services, but I wanted him to do it himself so that he would take full responsibility for what he had done. I wanted the mother to participate in turning him in to the authorities, so that she would take responsibility for not having protected her daughters from her husband's violence.

I had accomplished my goals for the second session.

The Third Session

My goals for the third session were simple: for the father to read to the family his letter to Protective Services, to give it to me to be mailed, and to begin a discussion about how relationships in the family could improve.

I started the session by saying to the girls, "Your parents came last time without you and made some decisions. Now they have something to show you." I turned to the father. "Did you bring it?"

"The letter?" asked Ken. "Hm-mm." He handed the letter to me.

"Would you like to read it to them?" I asked.

"Yes," he answered. "It's a letter addressed to the Protective Services Department":

> To Whom It May Concern:
>
> I would like to inform your office of a problem that my family has been experiencing. Laura and I have been married for twenty-one years. Five years ago, Laura and I had an argument during which I pushed her, causing her to fall on the floor where she was unconscious for about two minutes. Subsequently, episodes of violence occurred between me and my oldest daughter, Kristen, a seventeen-year-old. I recall

*three occasions when I struck Kristen with my open hand,
one time causing her lip to bleed and another when I smacked
her hard on the top of her head.*

*My little daughter, Caroline, has not escaped my violent
attacks. I hit Caroline on the leg with a closed fist one time
when we were in the car and on that same occasion I hit her
on the stomach as well, but my memory of this is not clear.
Only my youngest daughter, Sherry, has escaped physical
abuse at my hand.*

*Only recently with the help of counseling have I recog-
nized the gravity of my actions. I deeply regret the fact that
my wife and children have suffered physically because of my
inexcusable actions. Although family problems have not yet
been resolved, we are making progress toward that goal, and
I fervently believe that my family is no longer at risk of violent attacks from me.*

Sincerely,
Ken Jones

There was a silence when Ken stopped reading the letter. Then he
said to the girls, "This is something that I was asked to do and that
I think is an important thing to do to make sure that we all recognize the fact that this hitting of people is stopping, that it's not
going to happen again."

"If you send that somewhere," asked Kristen, "is it going to hurt
your career or something?" Here again she was showing her protectiveness toward her father, not just her mother. The letter could certainly seriously damage the father's career and his position in the
community.

"It's the truth," said Ken. "It's the way it is. It's what happened."

"Why does it need to be sent somewhere?" asked Kristen.

"I think it needs to be sent somewhere so that somebody else is
also aware of the problem," answered Ken.

"It's none of their business, really," complained Kristen belligerently.

"It is and it isn't," said Ken. "It depends on whether or not it's necessary for other people to know so that this doesn't ever happen again."

"Well, I mean," said Kristen, "what are they going to do?"

"I don't know what they're going to do," said the father. "Probably they'll send a social worker out to the house to see what's going on."

"They might," I said, "or they might not."

"You haven't actually mailed the letter, have you?" asked the mother.

"No, no," said Ken. "I just wrote it last night."

"So I will mail it today," I said.

"Is this the government that it's going to?" asked Laura.

"Hm-mm," answered Ken.

The mother began to cry. The girls looked very scared.

I turned to them. "It's against the law to hit somebody, so the honest thing when one has committed an act against the law is to report oneself. It's a protection for you and for your mother also, because should something ever happen again, the question from the Department of Social Services would be, was the mother an accomplice because she didn't report it. That's why it's very important for you to write it," I said to the mother, "and for it to be in your handwriting at the bottom of the letter, 'The above is true, and I agree with my husband in reporting this,' and sign your name to it because it protects you."

The letter was signed, and I mailed it. A couple of weeks later I received a phone call from a Protective Services worker who was not at all pleased and could not understand the therapeutic value of the father reporting himself, instead of my reporting him. I apologized and promised to continue with the therapy and to let them know if any new problem developed.

The Course of Therapy

I continued to work with the family, sometimes seeing them all together, sometimes meeting with the parents or with Kristen alone. There were no more episodes of violence. I focused on communication within the family and on the parents' relationship with their parents. Kristen's behavior improved, but, even though she had been admitted to the college of her choice, she said she wasn't sure she was ready for college and maybe that she should stay home.

I realized that Kristen couldn't leave her parents with their bad relationship. But every attempt I made at improving the marital relationship was like pulling an elephant. The father appeared interested in getting closer to his wife, but the mother rejected him and wouldn't explain why. I decided to do something unusual to improve the parents' marriage and to help Kristen to leave them.

Kristen Advises Her Father

I decided to invite only Kristen and her father to a session. I would speak first with Kristen alone, discussing with her how she would advise her father on how he could improve his marriage. Then the father would come into the session, and Kristen would give him her advice.

This intervention would accomplish several purposes. First, Kristen needed a ritual that would signify her transition to an adult life now that she was turning eighteen and about to go to college. Advising her father signified that she was not only considered an adult but was equal or even superior to her father in that she was advising him, and not the other way around. Second, it was important to break the intense bond that tied father and daughter together so that the father could be closer to his wife and so that Kristen could leave. If she advised him on how to win back his wife, Kristen would in effect be saying to him, 'She is your wife, not I. Be with her.' In the third place, for Kristen to become a woman she needed to be closer to her mother. In advising the father on how to win back his wife, Kristen would be putting herself in the mother's place in order to understand her, and, while identifying with her, she would feel closer.

I began by talking to Kristen alone. "What do you think your mother wants from your father?" I asked.

"I think she wants him to be himself and not be like. . . . I mean, I get the feeling like either he's himself and he just ignores everybody and stays at work, or else he's being fake and comes home and tries to be the family man, you know. And it's just annoying because it's not the way he is."

"So she would like him to be authentic," I said.

"Yeah, not be like, 'Laura, I brought you flowers,' because that's not him."

I handed Kristen a notepad. "You ought to make some notes of these things, so that you'll remember."

"He's just . . . ," Kristen continued. "I just think that they have too much of a business relationship. I mean, he'll come home and he'll be like, 'This needs cleaning, this needs doing, this needs. . . .' Eric, my friend, came over the other day and he was like, 'God, your dad! There's so much tension!' He just comes home and it's like. . . ." Kristen made a growling noise. "He just creates a lot of tension a lot of the time, and I think it bugs her, although she does it too, to an extent."

"So what you want to say is . . . ," I said.

"Cut the business relationship," said Kristen.

"What do you think that she would want? Do you think that she would want for him to say, 'Let's go and spend an evening alone?'"

"Yeah, I think he ought to spend time with her."

"Should he suggest that they go out to dinner?"

"Why don't they go on vacation?" asked Kristen. "I mean, if they just went out to dinner I could see them just talking about the kids, you know."

I was fascinated by how well Kristen knew her parents. "So write down," I said, "'Go out to dinner and don't talk about the kids.'"

"Yeah."

"Some of these things I have suggested myself," I added, "but I think that you have more power than I do."

"He's so authoritarian," reflected Kristen, "and so abrupt, like, rude a lot to her. He's like, 'She didn't balance the checkbook,' and gets all mad. I'm like, 'Give me a break—who cares if she didn't!' He's too . . . I think he just needs to be more mellow."

"How about if he asks for her opinion on things?" I suggested.

"Yeah."

"Ask for her opinion on at least two things a day?" I asked.

"No, I think that's trying too hard. I think it's got to be a little more natural. When he gets into trying too hard he really overdoes it, and I want to avoid that at all costs 'cause it will drive her up a tree." It was remarkable how well Kristen understood both her parents. Like every good scientist, the father was quite obsessive, so if he began to count, he would obsess forever.

Kristen continued, "I think he's sexist, actually. He always says he's not, but I think he is. I think he's like kind of chauvinistic."

"Well, let's think positive," I said.

"I think he should just erase everything and start over with her."

"And then do what with her? Put that down." I pointed to the notepad: "'Erase everything and start over.'"

"Maybe they should plan their next anniversary, like, not get married, but. . . ."

"Renew their marital vows," I said.

"Yeah, something like that."

"That's a great idea!" I exclaimed.

"Go on a big trip, something like a second honeymoon. Like after they work it all out. Give it a year to work it out."

"That's a great idea!"

"My dad is like so uneccentric," Kristen went on. "He's like so normal, it's annoying."

"Do something crazy?" I suggested.

"Yeah, he just needs to be less normal." She thought for a moment. "I think he should shave his beard."

"Oh, that would signify a big change!"

Kristen laughed. "He's not going to like that, but maybe if he's acting differently and also looks different. . . . I think it would take twenty years off. I think he looks at least twenty years older with a beard, 'cause he doesn't really have gray hair besides being bald, and his beard is totally gray. I think he looks about sixty or seventy, when he's only forty."

"No!" I laughed.

Kristen's recommendations were all wise and appropriate. She proceeded to discuss how her grandfather could be an appropriate role model for her father. "You can look at my grandparents and see that they are in love. My grandfather always tells stories about himself for hours and he's hysterical," she said. "He'll say, 'This little thing on this chair right here, she's my life.'"

"So remind him of them, because he's seen them many times," I said. "You have a great list of suggestions. I'll bring him in and you can advise him."

I brought the father in from the waiting room.

"I asked Kristen to help you with advice on how to win your wife over and how to charm her," I said, "how to seduce her, how to get her to like you again, because I think that's a problem."

"I agree," said Ken.

"I think you have been trying and not been able to get through, and I think that you've been frustrated," I said.

"Right."

"And I think that Kristen knows her very well, and she has some things that she can suggest to you in a kind, compassionate way," I emphasized, looking at Kristen, as a reminder that this was not about criticizing her father. "So she has a long list here."

"A long list?" said Ken. "Well, good. That's encouraging."

I turned to Kristen. "You can start wherever you want on the list and check off what you tell him and then give him the list."

"I'm all ears," said the father.

"Be what you want," began Kristen, "not what you think she wants. Like you'll look at her and you think 'I think she wants me to do this,' so you'll do it, and it's not like really coming from you. It's not like what you really want to say or do, but it seems like what you think she wants."

"Right," said Ken. "I'm aware of that one. Actually, that's an excellent point. I learned that one about a year ago. I'll try to practice it."

"Cut the business relationship," continued Kristen.

"OK," said the father.

I was thinking that it was remarkable how the father seemed to know precisely what Kristen was talking about.

She continued, "Spend more time with her and take her out to dinner, and don't talk about us, you know. Go somewhere really nice, or just to McDonald's, but take her out somewhere."

"That's a lot more difficult than you might imagine, but it's a good idea."

"It doesn't have to be," said Kristen.

"But it is. Not for me, but for her to find the time."

"No, it's not. If she complains just be like, 'Sorry, we're going out to dinner and you have to come.' You have to be a little more. . . . I mean, you'll sit there and you'll try something and if you're set back a little bit, you're like, 'Fine, forget it,' and just get mad. You have to be like, 'We're going out to dinner!'" exclaimed Kristen, gesturing enthusiastically with both arms. "'We really haven't spent any time together. I really want to spend time with you, so let's go out to dinner. The kids can wait; everything else can wait.'"

"OK."

"Relax, because you always seem a little uptight. Ask her for her opinion too, rather than just giving her your opinion on everything. And I think you should erase everything and start all over."

"Now that's a very, very important point right there," said Ken. "That's really extremely important. I agree wholeheartedly with you. I've been thinking about this for a long time; I've been thinking about this in my head."

"I think you should work on it the entire year," continued

Kristen, "and at your next anniversary you should get married again. I'm serious. You should tell her about it and like fix everything. 'We're going to get remarried!'" Kristen gestured with enthusiasm. "And I think that you should go to the Bahamas, or Hawaii, or France, or something, without any of us."

"She means a renewal of the marital vows," I said, "in the church and everything."

"Exactly, exactly," he said. "I know what you're saying."

"And have a big party and stuff," said Kristen.

"I'm not sure she'd marry me again, but go ahead," said Ken.

"She would," said Kristen, "seriously. Go on another honeymoon and go to like Paris. I mean, save your money. It's more important than a family vacation, 'cause I think just the two of you should go on vacation and not take the kids, not talk about the kids, not think about the kids. I'll be home, I can stay with them, I'll be going through college, and things will be fine."

I was certainly relieved to hear her say this.

"And I think that you ought to be less normal." They both laughed. "I'm serious, I mean do something crazy for her or with her. Like if you look at the family she came from, when her dad felt guilty for whatever reason, he'd walk downstairs and he'd be like, 'No, you're all too sick to go to school,' and he'd take them somewhere weird. And Brian with all his seaweed and his gadgets. She's used to all those bizarre things going on in the house, like Bob sitting there putting mice in her bed, you know."

"Yeah."

"And I think our house has gotten to a point where it's too normal. When I was little I remember that you guys were weird. Mom dressed weird, she wore these big huge bell-bottoms with the plaid, and you would dress up and play Prince Charming and Cinderella. You and Mom would do all these weird things. She would put on a wig, and you would be really strange. You don't do that any more. In second grade I remember being at a birthday party and talking about how gross boys were, and Mom grabbed Dad and started kissing him and said, 'They're not that bad.' I was so embarrassed I never wanted to go to school again.

"And I think you should come home from work more. You work too much, and when things get bad you run away to work instead of blowing it off. I think you should be less stubborn and less set in your ways and change your habits and be a friend. And stop the checkbook arguments and things like 'You don't have any gas in the car,' or 'Your checkbook's running out,' because she knows that and you know that. And I think you should shave your beard."

The father, who had been listening very attentively, laughed and stroked his beard. "OK?"

"I'm serious because I think you would look different, and I think you would look twenty years younger."

"It would represent a personality change," he said, "and a new start is what you're thinking."

"It would remind her more of the way you were before," said Kristen. "We were talking about patterns that you could follow, like people who have good relationships, like the Monroes. You know how strange and funny they are. And when they fight, they're honest with each other. Like Jim and Mary, too. Jim is pretty normal and structured in his life, like you. You are a lot alike. But with him and Mary, you know how they bicker, but they don't take it seriously—you know what I mean."

"Hm-mm, yeah," said Ken.

"They're really good with their arguments. They do it in front of everybody too. Like me and Caroline. I'm so close to Caroline that I'll be like 'Caroline, shut up, you're being a jerk!' and she'll be like 'Kristen, you shut up too!' And it'll be OK. I mean, we're honest and we can be really nasty, but when it's over, it's over and we worked it out, and it's kind of funny to us because we're so honest about it. Say what you think but not in such a heavy way. I mean, be honest but don't drag it so deep and be like, 'This is upsetting me—the den is messy.' You know, just be like, 'The den's a mess,' you know. It doesn't have to be blaming her; don't blame people.

Like Grandfather. Grandfather is hysterical. We were sitting in the den and you know how Grandfather always carries out discussions?"

"To himself, yes."

"Well, he was talking to us and he said, 'You know, if I had never found this one next to me, I would have never gotten married.' And they're just really romantic. She'll sit on his lap, and he'll be like, 'Ma, you're about to break my legs,' and she'll turn around and swat him with something. He was like flirting with the waitress, and she rolled her eyes and he said, 'But none of them are as pretty as you, Ma.' They're really cute, they've gotten adorable. They have a great relationship they may not have had before, but I think now, because Nana has gotten more independent and Grandfather's gotten less dogmatic, they have one of the best relationships ever."

Kristen closed her notepad, and I said, "What do you think of that? She's pretty smart, huh?" I was deeply impressed by Kristen's insight into her parents' relationship and by her understanding of what makes a good marriage.

"Yeah," said her father, "she's a smart kid. Those are all very good ideas, very good ideas, and I appreciate very much your thinking about it. It helped me."

"I'll make a copy for you, a copy for her, and a copy for me," I said.

This session was a turning point in the therapy. The father renewed his efforts with great enthusiasm, and soon the couple was going away for weekends, going out with friends, and enjoying each other more. Yet there was still tension in the relationship.

The next turning point was after Kristen went off to college. Laura surprised me by suddenly announcing that she had gotten a job and not just any job, but a very interesting, well-paying one. The fact that she was now away from the home, working all day, drastically changed her relationship with her husband and with the children. Their expectations of her had to change, her everyday life became more like her husband's, and she had new and interesting things to talk about. I had often thought during the therapy that I wanted to advise her to go to work, but she seemed so sensitive about being a housewife that I was afraid to offend her with the suggestion. So I was very pleased to hear that she had made this decision on her own.

The Steps

What steps can be generalized from this therapy of social action to other cases where a father is physically abusive toward an adolescent child?

Step 1. Bring the whole family together, and find out about all the incidents of violence: when, where, how, why, what happened before, and what happened after. The more serious the violence, the more extended family should be brought in so that the violence is made public to the whole family. Prevent the parents from minimizing the father's violence.

Step 2. Ask the father why what he did was wrong, and, if he doesn't understand, make sure that the family makes it very clear to him. If you doubt that the father understands, bring in extended family and members of the community to explain. Violence involves a network of people including not just the victimizer and the victim but all those who are involved with them. A therapy of social action must include at least the most important part of this network.

The first step in preventing future violence is for the victimizer and the family to understand that violence is wrong and should be prevented. A therapy of social action is based on a clear sense of ethics, of what is right and wrong. Violence against children is always wrong. The therapist must make sure that the whole family understands this.

Step 3. Ask the father about who is responsible for his violence. Make sure he takes full responsibility without blaming anyone. If he doesn't, bring to bear the pressure of extended family and community. He must not only believe he is responsible; he must verbally express it.

A therapy of social action is a therapy of social responsibility. Our first responsibility is to protect and not abuse our children. The therapist must be clear that an important goal of therapy is to protect the human rights of children and that what is morally right is also therapeutic. It's morally right for the father to take full responsibility for his violence, without excuses.

Step 4. Ask the father to apologize sincerely to each child he has hurt. Make sure the family agrees that the apology is sincere. If the violence is extreme, he should apologize on his knees, as a posture of repentance. You might want to ask the father to do an act of reparation for the child. Apologies and reparation are part of taking responsibility for one's actions and, therefore, an essential component of a therapy of social action.

Step 5. Ask the father to report himself to Protective Services. This is more therapeutic than if you report him because it means that he takes full responsibility for his actions.

Step 6. Often a child who has been abused by a parent behaves in self-destructive ways. If that is the case, intervene to prevent suicide and other self-destructive behaviors. See the child alone, and encourage him in the direction of the fulfillment of a dream, of something to look forward to that you can help arrange.

Step 7. Explore the link between the father's violence and marital problems. There usually is such a link, and a phase of marital therapy is required.

Step 8. Change the meaning of the violent behavior so that instead of expressing power, it expresses impotence. Change the metaphor of violence in a way that is significant to each particular father.

Step 9. Find out about violence in previous generations. Motivate the parents to prevent violence from continuing in the present. You might have to work on the parents' relationship with their parents.

Step 10. Do something special to improve the relationship between the father and the abused child, especially in the direction of developing the father's appreciation of that particular child.

. . . .

4

The Knife in Her Heart

Cloé Madanes with James P. Keim

A man called the Family Therapy Institute from jail where he was serving a sentence for sexually molesting his daughter. He had been ordered by the court to therapy but was dissatisfied with the prison therapist. Some of the other inmates had told him that we were the best therapists in the area, so he had decided to try us. Now he was in a work release program, employed during the day as an elevator repairman and coming back to prison in the evening. He thought he could get permission to come to therapy once a week between finishing work and going back to jail.

Jim Keim wanted to do the therapy, and I decided to be his consultant behind the one-way mirror, observing the sessions and making suggestions as to how the therapy could proceed. I was interested in the man's problem and suspected he was in great despair, since he was arranging therapy in difficult circumstances.

Goals

Jim and I met before the first session to discuss our goals. The man, Ray, was twenty-nine years old; his daughter was eight, and his son was nine. That was all we knew. Yet we already had certain goals:

1. We wanted to encourage Ray to take full responsibility for the sexual abuse. No matter what the circumstances, abusing his daughter was his sole responsibility. No one else was to blame.

2. Sexual abuse by a father of a child is a particularly heinous crime because in human beings, sexuality and spirituality are related. When this attack comes from a most trusted person, a father on whom the child depends for life sustenance, the spiritual suffering is extremely painful. This spiritual pain not only affects the child but also the father, because it is so horrible to inflict this pain on another human being, particularly on one's own child. We had to address this spiritual pain in the therapy. A therapy of social action is a holistic approach that takes into account the social, the psychological, and the spiritual components of the person.

3. Ray needed not only to understand the depth of the pain he had inflicted; he had to express to his daughter the depth of his sorrow and repentance for having inflicted this pain. The child had to know that the father understood the spiritual pain that he caused, that he took full responsibility, and that he was profoundly sorry. This was the first step toward helping her heal, and to help his daughter heal from the wounds he had given her had to be Ray's goal.

   We didn't know yet how we would be able to accomplish this goal, since in these cases there is usually a restraining order forbidding the father from being in the presence of his daughter.

4. While encouraging Ray to take responsibility for the abuse, Jim also had to be concerned about preventing suicide. There is a high incidence of suicide among sex offenders, so we had to assume that Ray might be suicidal. We were particularly concerned because, as an elevator repairman, Ray had ample opportunity to kill himself swiftly and painlessly.

   In a therapy of social action every individual is valuable. Every person, no matter what he has done, has the possibility of self-determination, of choosing to do the right thing in the future, of turning his life around for the better for himself and for society. It was important to encourage Ray to stay alive, not only to save his life but for the sake of his daughter. If he killed himself, his daughter might blame herself for his death, which would be a catastrophic event for her.

5. To keep Ray alive, Jim needed to help him find meaning in life, in spite of the crime he had committed. He had to have a goal that transcended him. He had to live, no matter how painfully, because there were things he had to do. He had to do reparation to his children for the harm he had caused them: to his daughter, for sexually molesting her; to his son, for abusing his sister. This reparation would involve the rest of his life, and he had to stay alive to do it.

In a therapy of social action, the individual is required to take responsibility, not just for his past but for his future actions. The concept of self-determination includes making up for one's mistakes and wrongdoing. No matter what the circumstances, there is always the power to choose. One can always choose to do reparation to correct as much as possible the harm that was inflicted.

The First Session: Sorrow

Jim and I were particularly concerned about preventing suicide because the first session was taking place in December, close to Christmas, when a large number of suicides typically occur. So Jim decided to start the session by asking how Ray was planning to spend Christmas day.

Ray walked into the therapy room and sat heavily on the sofa. He was a big chunk of a man, a Viking type with strawberry blond hair, blond beard, a ruddy complexion, and the body of an over-weight football player (later we learned that he had actually been a football player in college, where he had almost graduated as an engineer). In contrast, Jim, who was close in age to Ray, looked small and pale, with thinning dark hair, studious round glasses, and a Freudian beard.

Introductions had obviously happened in the waiting room, because as they sat down, Jim said, "Can you go to Christmas dinner and that sort of thing?"

"No," answered Ray.

"No kidding, that's terrible!" said Jim.

"Well, it comes, I guess, with the situation," said Ray, tense, sad, looking straight ahead, not making eye contact.

"The jail sentence is really the minimal part," Ray continued. "Everything that happened before the sentencing was really the hardest part. That's what I'm trying to deal with right now."

When we met before the session, I had told Jim that it probably would be difficult for Ray to talk about what he had done to his daughter. Yet he had to talk about it. But if Jim made the conversation less painful, it would be easier to conduct the therapy because he would be more inclined to like Jim. I assumed that a man who had committed such a despicable act probably had quite a complicated history, so I suggested that Jim continue the session by asking Ray to tell him the "story" of his life. That way Ray didn't have to begin with the abuse of his daughter. He could start wherever he wanted to in his life, but, in telling a "story," he would have to give some meaning to his life. There would have to be a sequence: a beginning that led to certain events, events that had consequences, and so on.

Since a primary effort in Ray's therapy would be to give meaning to his life, we could begin by asking what sense he could make of his life now. Jim didn't ask the question quite in the right way, yet the answer was significant.

"Tell me about your life," said Jim.

"Well, I had two kids," said Ray, "a son and a daughter from my previous marriage. I was married in '81, got divorced or separated about four and a half years later. I met my second wife in '88. So I had the children by myself for a couple of years. My first wife didn't really have a lot of interest in the kids. I guess that's why she didn't take them right off the bat. I guess she was at a point in her life when she didn't really want them."

As Ray talked, I was thinking how important the children were to him. When asked about his life, he started right off with his children.

"We had a rough marriage," continued Ray. Later on I understood that by "rough," Ray meant that he was horribly violent with his first wife. "And I guess I didn't really know whether I was ready to raise two kids by myself. My daughter was three; my son was four. So I had them until I met my girlfriend who became my wife. . . . She actually did a fantastic job, was a fantastic mother to those kids. One of the hardest things of what happened with all this is what's happened to her. I had a joint custody sort of thing with my ex-wife. She could have seen the kids as much as she wanted, but she didn't do that. She started seeing them more regularly only a year ago, once every two weeks. My son is an extremely bright kid. My daughter was born with a cleft palate. I got her through the major surgeries."

"How many of them did she have?" asked Jim. Nothing that Jim said in this therapy was casual conversation. Every word was directed to fulfilling our goals for Ray. When Jim asks at this point about how many operations, he is emphasizing that Ray abused a child who had already suffered so much.

"She had her first operation at two months, the second one at five months. . . . She's had a total of five operations. One was an ear operation."

"Wow, so it was pretty extensive."

"Yeah, she was a complete cleft palate."

"So she had no palate between her mouth and her nasal cavity."

"She was a single; she wasn't a bilateral. It worked out pretty good. The plastic surgeon did a fantastic job. I mean, to look at her, you could see that she's had it, but it's not offensive, just a slight scar. At this point, her speech is probably the biggest impediment she's working on. Her hearing is coming along; she's hearing pretty good. And she's got her first set of orthodontics in right now. My son's nine now, and she's eight. Other than that, in terms of the actual abuse, I never did anything to my son. The abuse of my daughter . . . I had a few isolated instances in the end of '86. Then it stopped and didn't begin again until about '89. It's like, once you get into that thing, it's like you know you need help, but you're trapped on how you can get it." Ray gestured with his arms and hands as if he were in an invisible trap, the expression on his face was pained, frustrated. He seemed oblivious to Jim, looking into himself.

"Finally my daughter . . . ," he went on. "I hadn't done anything for a couple of months. . . . And she just told my wife [her step-mother]. My wife confronted me with it, and I wasn't really sure what I was going to do at the time. It seemed at least it was out, and I could talk to someone about it, where before I was trapped. I wanted to tell someone about it, but then I'd say, 'I can stop this on my own.' Then I got to the point where I realized that I was no longer in control of myself at all.

"I always thought it was really stress related. When things were really bad for me, when I look back now, that's when these things would occur. At that time I was having a lot of problems in my marriage and things like that, a lot of stress at work. When things between me and my wife were pretty good, we made up after an argument, then I'd stop the behavior almost as if it had never happened. And one of the most puzzling things for me was how I was ever able to go back into this cycle.

"So anyway, my wife told my mother about it. We sat down to talk, and my mother was worried at the time about me killing myself. She told me to go down to Eastwood Hospital. I saw the nurse on psychiatric duty and told her what happened. Well, by the time I got home, Social Services was there. I moved out of the house; I did everything to the letter of what they wanted me to do. The problem was, the kids went over to my ex-wife's house two weeks afterwards, and my daughter told her. And my ex-wife just kept the kids, took me to court, and now . . . I'm so far out of the picture for those two that if I ever see them again, it'll be amazing to me."

There was total despair in Ray's voice. "I haven't seen either one of my children since February. Haven't talked to them. I almost got thrown in jail once for trying to talk to them, and I'm at a point now where I don't really know what to do. I don't really see a time in the foreseeable future when I can get back with my kids. I don't see how it can happen. I wasn't one of the fortunate guys who had a group of kids and a family who stayed together, who even if they're outside of the house they have a hope of getting back in."

Listening to Ray, I realized how much he loved his daughter. It would have been naive to assume otherwise. Like many other sex offenders, he was confused as to what is love and what is violence. He could love his daughter and abuse her at the same time. This confusion between love and violence had probably developed because Ray, himself, had been abused as a child by someone who was supposed to love him. We needed to find out who that person was, not because it would in any way justify Ray's behavior (many children who are abused never become abusers—there is a choice to be made) but because we needed to "exorcise" that memory, get it out of Ray's system, so that he could no longer love and at the same time exert violence.

Jim didn't want Ray to continue with the theme of hopelessness. If he was to stay alive, he had to be hopeful for a better future. "Well, I'll tell you," said Jim, "a lot of times guys come in with your situation, and they have no expectation that they'll ever see their kids, that they'll be able to apologize, or do something in some way to help the situation. They feel so frustrated. . . . But we usually find some ways.

"I see you're in a lot of pain over this. But for life to make sense, some good has to come of this pain. Someone has to be better off. Something constructive should come out of this, and I'd like to help you with that. I don't know if your friends told you this, but we often work toward that. I can see that this is something that's really tearing your soul apart. You've got to do something about it."

Jim had begun to introduce the idea of spiritual pain, of apology, and of reparation.

"In our group therapy in jail, there's a dozen men," said Ray, "who, no matter how extreme what they did, as long as they made some agreement with the state's attorney that they would get some therapy—everything they did is erased. I went through the court, the trial, the charging, I agreed to the therapy, and I was thrown in jail. In a sense, doing the time is not really hard. It's a joke, really, to consider that punishment. It's just the hopelessness of it all. The system did what it was supposed to do, but I had these kids for five years, and they didn't even consider that. I haven't seen these kids now . . . " (his voice was breaking with emotion as he continued) ". . . specially my son. . . . He's been in therapy to deal with the shift, moving homes, but, you know, I never abused him. We had a pretty good relationship. And . . . this counseling I'm with now, I'm not really sure that I'm going to get any farther with it. I'm at a point where I'm so bitter toward everything that's happened."

Jim could see that Ray was attempting to blame the court system for his misfortune. As with most sex offenders, he wanted to put responsibility outside of himself. He had to be led back to being responsible for his own actions. Yet it was crucial to encourage hopefulness. The hopelessness and bitterness that Ray was expressing were warning signals that a suicide attempt was possible. Jim took one word that Ray had used—the *system*—and turned it around, giving it a different meaning, giving a goal to Ray's life that was almost heroic:

"Well, I'll tell ya," said Jim, "sometimes the way the system works is almost like a filtration system. Only the people who most want to have a relationship with their kids and most want to go on with their lives, only those who most want to help their children, will have a relationship with their kids. And I think you're that kind of guy. I think, just as you said, that jail isn't bad. What's bad is the pain of what you did and of being away from your kids, wanting to have a relationship with them. And you'd do just about anything for them, to let them know how sorry you are."

"I am," whispered Ray.

Jim had taken him back to his responsibility and his pain, yet given him hope and emphasized once again the need to apologize and express repentance.

"How many years have you been a father to them?" asked Jim.

"Nine, ten years."

"You don't stop being a father by being put in jail."

"Well, I understand I've got to be away from them. . . ," said Ray, who was probably repeating the bad advice he had received from others. To stay away from the children would only add insult to injury. It would mean that Ray had not only abused his daughter; he would also abandon her and her brother. Our plan was the opposite. We wanted to organize Ray to do reparation to his children for the rest of his life.

There is no court order that can permanently separate a parent from a child if they don't want to be separate. When Ray's daughter reached the age of eighteen, chances were she would look for her father and find him. Then they would have a relationship without the influence of a therapist. Our goal was to bring them together now and correct the relationship so that the child could have a father who cared for her instead of one who raped her.

"I'll tell ya," said Jim, "your children need to figure out and reconcile with what happened, and they need to know what their future is with you. Because children have this picture of their father in their head, they have to know how he's doing. And they may be pissed at that father, they may be angry, they might also love him . . . , and yet in some part of their brain they're always thinking about their parents. And for their sake you have to do what you have to do. Let me ask you, and I'm sure in therapy you've talked about this time and time again. But let me ask you, what exactly did you do?"

"I fondled my daughter; I performed oral sex on my daughter. I never penetrated her either with my finger or intercourse, but I did simulate it—I'd turn her around so that she couldn't see—by using her legs. That was really it."

"Did it start that way or. . . ."

"At the beginning I basically had her masturbate me. I had her hand on me, and I used her hand to masturbate under the covers."

"Did you sleep together at the time?"

"No. My relationship with my first wife was kind of a strange ritual of violence and sex. I know back in '86 I was pretty far out. She left, and for a period of time after she left, there was a kind of relief, and I found myself doing better after she'd gone. The abuse didn't happen again until '89. Then it just started out fondling. And it was toward December or November of '90 that I started simulating intercourse with her. I would turn her around so that she never really saw me. I would just do that, I guess, until I got off. It was weird. I was fantasizing about having a relationship with my ex-wife.

"When I look back, I don't think I was ever attracted to my daughter as a child. That's one of the things I have a problem dealing with too. It's that I've never been attracted to children. The idea to touch a child had been no more in my mind than . . . my next door neighbor's child, or any child I've ever seen, you know. Having sex with a child was as sick to me then basically as it is to me now. I was able to basically convert my daughter into an adult through fantasy."

Studies on sex offenders suggest that there is one type, like Ray, who will only molest the daughter of a particular woman that he is obsessed with. The child represents the mother in the man's mind.

"Whenever problems that were in my life dissipated for a period of time," continued Ray, "whether for a couple of weeks or whatever, I'd stop the behavior and just go back to being father and daughter, with everything about as normal as can be. Except, looking back, for her it must have been a Dr. Jekyll and Mr. Hyde sort of thing—that must have been the worst thing, you know. 'Daddy's been having some strange behavior from time to time.'

"I usually had it set up where it got to the point that it was almost planned. My wife worked late on Friday nights, and that's when the abuse would occur. There was a period of time when I'd push myself away from it as far as I could, but it was almost like I was driven to it, like a compulsion. Then I would do it, and it was . . . man . . . like, swoosh, I would fall into a black hole. I mean, for about two days afterwards it was, 'What the hell is wrong with me? What is wrong with me?' And I knew I needed help. I wanted to get help, but I didn't want all this to happen."

"What is the most painful memory for you?" said Jim. He wanted to make the pain very concrete for Ray, so there would be no denial.

"I think the most painful memory for me is the earliest abuse back in '86 for the simple reason of her age. I remember in the group they said, 'How big was she?' and I just burst out crying. I couldn't believe I had done that. It's really painful to me, specially because she had so many things to overcome as it was, her cleft palate, her speech and all that. And I found myself, from early on, really protecting this kid, because I knew that there would be a period of time in school when kids would start making fun of the way she talked and things like that. And I used to be really offended when I'd be at work or something and someone would make a crack about people with a hare lip. It hurt me because my daughter had that," he pounded his chest for emphasis. "So that's the biggest thing that hurts in my own life, is that I did so much in the beginning to protect this kid, and I ended up abusing her."

"How tall was she when it started?" asked Jim, not letting Ray get away from the concrete memory.

"That tall," said Ray, gesturing with his hand about three feet off the floor, and then holding his head in his hands in a gesture of despair.

"That must be a painful memory."

"It's painful, because . . . man . . . of all the things I could have done wrong, why did it have to be . . . why did I have to. . . . I mean, we were taught how compulsive behavior takes many forms:

alcohol, drug abuse, jogging, whatever. Why couldn't I have become
an alcoholic, why didn't I abuse drugs? You know, I don't do drugs;
I don't drink. Why did this have to be my outlet? It's totally blown
away any image I ever had of myself as a human being. I mean, how
do you go on with life after you've done something like this? How
do you face yourself on a day-to-day basis?

"In jail it's different. For one thing, they don't know what I'm in
there for. I was lucky enough that mine didn't make the papers, and
in jail you basically put up a facade anyway. You find some way to
be hard; you find some way of coping with the people in there. But
I found myself thinking about this . . . and it never leaves me . . . it
never leaves me . . . and it drives me crazy. I see my wife. . . . I see
her because here she's stuck right in the middle of this! She lost her
kids, and I'm in jail. [The judge had given custody of the children
to the first wife, who made it difficult for the second wife to see
them.] I mean, through no fault of her own other than that she happened to be married to me. She lost her two kids . . . and wham!
The guilt associated with that. . . . How does the pain ever go
away?"

"The pain can change," said Jim. This was precisely the right
thing to say. To suggest that the pain could go away would have
been false optimism. But the pain certainly would change, just as
everything else constantly changes. "You're in a situation now," continued Jim, "where it's very difficult for you to do what a person
who's not in jail could do to start fixing things. Yet there are some
things you could do that maybe I can help you with. But if you can't
do something positive with the pain that you have, it's going to eat
you up."

"It is eating me up," said Ray. "I've spent the last six months
wondering which day it would be when I just decided the hell with
it and either jumped off the building I was working on, electrocuted
myself, or. . . ."

"You know whom that would be the worst thing for?"

"I know, I've heard that too. . . ."

"Your kids."

"I know, I've heard that, but it gets to a point, when you've been away from them that long, where you don't hear from them, you don't know what's going on with them. . . ."

"You haven't told me about no-contact orders from the court or that kind of stuff, but the best thing for your kids at this point is to take some steps toward helping them heal." No one could help the children heal as effectively as the father who had hurt them. This had to be the goal that would give meaning to Ray's life. "And they need to see that, because in your head you have kind of a picture gallery. There's a photo of your dad and a photo of your mom, and you're born with that. That's why children have to know what their parents were like when they were young. Your kids will always need to know what's going on, whether you love them, whether you care for them, whether you care for their future, whether despite the bad things you've done and the mistakes you've made, you'll be able to protect them in the future. In how many months are you going to be out?"

"Probably August next year."

"And how old will your children be?"

"Nine and ten."

"So they have nine or ten years left of being teenagers when you come out. And let's say by then you only have a fraction of the time that you would like with them, still that's something. Some people in your position would be tempted to just blow them off. Some people in your position wouldn't know any better and would say, 'They're better off if I just don't contact them again, if I don't even live in this country any more.' But nothing could be worse for them. You've made your mistakes and hurt your kids, but the worst thing you could do to them now would be to hurt them more. And the only thing that you can morally do is to help them, because despite everything that's happened they still need you as a father.

"You know the teenage years are the most difficult," Jim went on. "When they're seventeen and eighteen they're going to be exposed to all sorts of dangerous things and dangerous people, and they're going to need you. You might make the difference between their surviving and their not surviving. There's crack out there, there's AIDS out there, and not only that, it's a different economy now, which means, financially speaking, you're probably going to be able to help their quality of life for years to come. And I'm not only talking about child support. I'm talking about the difference between them going to college and not going to college. A lot of this is going to be depending on you.

"It's almost like a test to see how badly you want to be a parent. All sorts of things are going to be out there to prevent you from being a parent. The real test is: are you going to have the guts to do what it takes?"

Once again, Jim makes the task ahead for Ray almost heroic, as a way of dramatically countering his suicidal ideas.

"It's one thing to say, yeah, I'm going to fight it all out," said Ray. "And it's another thing to. . . ."

"It's another thing to fight it out."

"The legal process, the battles with my ex-wife. . . ."

"Yeah."

"At this point in time she'd probably rather see me shot."

"She might well feel that way, and I'm sure she's pissed at you with justification. But when those kids are eighteen, she's going to need you. This is going to take some time, but I'd like to stick with you until after you have a relationship with your kids. Because, to be frank, rolling around in your own pain is going to do nothing for you. It's taking some real steps that will make a difference. You're limited right now, but the important thing is doing some things, in some small way, making up, not completely, but taking some steps. And I think you care that much about your kids. When you're depressed and think there's nothing out there, you've got to reach down inside and find that love for your kids, because that's the only thing you have to work for. There may be some other things, and we can talk about it, but when it comes down to it, your most important role in life is being a father."

"And I failed that role."

"You haven't. It goes on. It's not a role that can be taken away from you."

"It was taken away from me."

"If it was taken away from you, your kids wouldn't be thinking about you, and I promise you they are. And I tell you I'm worried about you. You've put a lot of energy into your kids, and if you start getting mixed up in your head like you're not a father any more or that they're not thinking about you, that worries me. No one is going to fill your place. No one is going to be a real father to your daughter except you. That's all there is to it. There's nothing that can make a person come into the situation and say, 'Hi, gee, I feel like I've always taken care of you. I feel like I stood by your side during those five surgeries.' There's nothing, no one's going to fill your place, not with your daughter, not with your son."

"It's just hard to see that now, that's all."

"Hey, it's my job to point out those things which are difficult to see right now!" Once again Jim said precisely the right thing, taking responsibility for the therapy. Then he changed the subject: "How about your wife? How are things with her?"

"They've gotten better. They go up and down. The first month I got put in jail I didn't really think there was any marriage left, but. . . ."

"Would you like her to come here also?"

"I don't think there's any way she'd come in here."

"Let me invite her," said Jim.

With that, the session ended. We had accomplished all our goals for the first session.

The Second Session: Repentance

Jim spoke with Ray's wife, Shirley, and invited her to come to the next session. Shirley said she was planning to divorce Ray and had no interest in participating in the therapy. Jim asked her to come just once, so that Ray could say certain things to her in Jim's presence that were necessary for the therapy. She didn't need to answer or to speak. Finally, she agreed to come.

Our goal for this session was to have Ray express his deep sorrow and repentance for how he hurt Shirley by abusing her stepchild. We would have preferred to gather the whole family together for an apology session, including the children and the biological mother, but this was not possible. There was a court order forbidding Ray to be in the presence of his children, and his ex-wife refused to see or speak to him. Jim began to work to obtain permission from the court to have one session where Ray could apologize to his daughter. But in the meantime we needed to bring someone else who was very significant and who would have wanted to protect the child, to see just how sincere Ray was in his apology. We needed to see the wife's reaction and hear her opinion as to whether he was truly repentant.

The expression of repentance to family members is essential to a therapy of social action, because without it there is no way of knowing that the offender truly accepts the wrongfulness of his actions and, therefore, no guarantee that the crime will not be repeated. And only the people who know the offender very well can tell whether his repentance is truly sincere.

Shirley's situation was particularly sad. When she married Ray, she became so fond of the children that she decided that she didn't need to have any children of her own, so she had her tubes tied. When the sexual abuse was discovered, Ray's ex-wife went to court and took custody of the children, so Shirley lost the children that she had raised and loved. Now she couldn't have any children at all.

When Shirley walked into the room, I was surprised to see how beautiful she was. With long, straight, dark hair, big dark eyes, a pale complexion, and a sharp nose, there was a certain resemblance to Greta Garbo. It was strange to think that Ray was using a child for sex while he was married to this woman.

Jim said to Ray, "I'd like you to tell Shirley how sorry you are for the pain you've caused her. You've taken away her children, and now she can't have any more children. You've taken away her household. You've taken away from her everything that she had dear to her life. The pain that you've caused her is a spiritual pain, a pain that's at the very core of us. I'd like you to get on your knees in front of Shirley and speak to the spirit, where the injury is. Not only to Shirley's injury, but to your injury as well, because that's also what you're speaking to, to the injury in yourself."

Ray stood up slowly and got on his knees in front of Shirley, his head down. "I'm sorry for all I've done to you, for taking those kids away from you. . . . I'm sorry. . . ." He began to quietly cry and his voice became unintelligible. He stayed in this posture for more than twenty minutes, crying as he said to Shirley words that Jim and I could not hear. She cried silently as he spoke.

Finally Jim asked him to sit back on the couch. He said, "You'll have a chance to tell your kids how bad you feel. I'll make sure of that. They need to see that with your pain you understand the pain that they're feeling, that you understand their spiritual pain, that you understand the pain in their heart that you've caused. Did you feel, Shirley, that Ray understands that pain?"

"Hm-mm."

"And your children will understand too," said Jim. He turned to Shirley: "Do you believe that Ray is truly repentant?"

"Yes," whispered Shirley, drying the tears that were rolling down her cheeks.

Jim turned to Ray: "Shirley needs to hear that even if she doesn't choose to take you back, that you will make sure for the rest of your life that you will help her to see the kids. She has to understand that your wish to help her is unconditional and you don't intend it as a bribe—that no matter what, for the rest of your life, you will try to help her to see the children."

"I want you to be able to see them," said Ray, "no matter whether we're together or whether we're apart, and I do love you. I will take care of you. Whatever happens, I will always want you to be able to see the kids, no matter if you have a relationship with me or not. You're a part of them, a part of their lives. I don't want to see that go away." He turned to Jim: "I will make it up to her. I owe it to her and the kids."

"That's all that counts," said Jim.

Ray said, "That's all that's there."

The Third Session: Apology

At the end of the second session, Jim had asked Ray to write a letter of apology to his daughter, Rosemary, and to bring it to the next session. Ray read it out loud for Jim:

Dear Rosemary,

I want you to know that I do love you, that I want to be a part of your life. I have done some very bad things to you. These are things you are in no way responsible for. I used you to meet my needs, and I'm sorry about how that made you feel. I'm sorry that I was the main person in your life and I let you down.

I know what I did was wrong. It was unjustified. I'm sorry that you have felt responsible for what was done to you, and probably still do. You did absolutely nothing wrong. I was the adult and any wrongdoing was my fault. I love you and I wish that I was a better Dad to you.

I do not want you to hate me for the rest of your life. People can change. I want to make up for all the years I was not a good Dad to you, and I want you to hold your head up, because nothing that was a result of my abuse was your fault.

I'm sorry that I lost you for this period of time that we were separated. You did the right thing about telling what was wrong. Nobody has any right to abuse you, including me. I'd like to be a better father to you.

"That is very good," said Jim. "It sounds like it comes exactly from your heart."

"It's exactly what I want to say."

"That's right. Let me shake your hand."

Both Rosemary and her brother Tom had an individual therapist, and Ray was paying for their therapy. When Jim had asked the judge for permission for an apology session with the children, he was told that the permission would only be granted if the two psychologists agreed. Both had absolutely refused, saying that the children were not ready to see him. It's curious that children who see their father every day all their lives suddenly are not capable of looking at him after the abuse is discovered. It was because the personal apology was not possible that Jim had asked Ray to write the letter.

Jim planned to continue attempting to have a session with the children, but in the meantime other issues had to be dealt with in therapy. Jim had spoken with Ray's first wife, Vicky, to ask her to come in to a session. She had refused but talked to Jim about how extremely violent Ray had been with her during their marriage. He had beat her so violently, even during the pregnancies of the two children, that she had even partially lost sight in one eye. We knew that for Ray to be rehabilitated, we had to stop not just the sexual abuse but also his violence. So the focus of the next sessions would be on violence.

The Fourth Session: Responsibility

Jim asked Ray to talk about the earliest episode that he could remember when he had been extremely violent. Ray said that when he first got married, he and his wife had a roommate with whom he had quarreled.

"So we got in an argument, and I can remember, he just kept pushing the issue," said Ray, pointing his finger and pushing aggressively in the air, "telling me he was going to get his father, this lawyer, to get him off of paying the rent somehow, and really stick it to me. And he was tired of living with me and my wife. And I remember I was saying, 'Man, just . . . just leave it . . . shut up,' but he kept pushing me and pushing me and pushing me." Ray gestured again with his finger. "Finally I just went off. He ended getting about eight stitches above his eye and a concussion, I guess 'cause I kept hitting him in the temple. I don't even remember how many times I hit him. It happened during a period of about thirty seconds."

"It sounds really violent," said Jim.

"It was. It was just like I remember that movie *The Incredible Hulk*; it was just like that. I remember I just started trembling and I felt this adrenaline pumping through my body. I kept telling him to just leave me alone, and he just kept pushing me, so I felt like an animal in a cage that's been prodded one too many times."

I could see that the problem Ray had was typical of violent men. He glorified violence. When he was violent, he turned into the Incredible Hulk, a television character who is a mild-mannered physician until he witnesses an injustice. Then he turns into a green monster with supernatural strength and punishes the wrongdoers, restoring justice. In Ray's mind, the Incredible Hulk was Ray's metaphor for violence: idealized, "macho," appropriate behavior. If we were to change Ray, we had to change this metaphor.

"Where did it come from?" asked Jim.

"What do you mean?"

"Some people are violent because that's just their personality. But that's not your personality. In other words, sometimes people go on automatic pilot. You know, tired, stressed out, sometimes a person goes on an automatic kind of mode. It's not an excuse, but when you're on automatic, there's kind of an 'out to lunch' setting that you go on, and that comes from somewhere. In other words, you follow an example of some kind. And that's not an excuse, of course, but I'm wondering where it came from."

Jim had begun to introduce the idea that Ray's violence was alien to him, incongruous with his personality, inserted into him like a program into a computer. If we could identify this "program-mer" as someone despicable in Ray's life, then the violence would itself become a despicable act. But Ray responded with an idealized view of the origin of his violence. It came from his father, whom he greatly admired. His father had recently moved to another country and had not come back or offered any support to Ray during his predicament.

"My father's one of these extremely laid-back people, you know," said Ray, "the type of person who gets along with everybody. He can come to a job and have like twenty friends in one day. But he's also the type of person you don't back into a corner, because until he comes out of the corner he's not going to tell you that anything's bothering him in any way, but eventually he's going to come out of the corner and he'll go off, just like an atomic bomb. My mother is also like that in a way. I got in a lot of fights with my mom because every time I came in late at night, we always had a big fight. It was always one of those deals when I was about to get in bed and she'd come down and say, 'Where've you been?'" Ray continued talking for a while about his mother's bad temper.

"It's a bad tradition in your family," said Jim, "going out of con-trol. How did the violence with your first wife get started?"

"The first time I ever hit her was a kind of response. She hit me. . . . I was driving down the road. We were fighting about some-thing. I can't even remember what it was, and I told her, 'Shut up, bitch,' which is something I never, I never usually addressed her that way. She had a thing about being called a bitch. I don't know why—it was just that one thing. And I don't know why but she slapped me while I'm driving, and it was like a reflex. I just went 'pap!'" He gestured with his arm as if slapping someone with the back of his hand. "And you know, I remember, it was weird, it was like a . . . like a reflex, like there was no other way I could have responded to that."

"What's the worst thing you ever did to her?"

"The worst thing I ever did was probably the last thing I ever did to her. I grabbed her by the back of the head and slammed her face into a table and then. . . ."

"That's scary."

"Yeah. And then, basically kicked her and threw her down. Almost immediately after, after the main part of the violence was over, it would be like I was normal again, looking down at this damage. I'd try to make it up to her, and then. . . ."

"That's frightening."

"And then usually we'd end up making up, and usually have sex. And it just became a pattern: violence before these sexual episodes."

"So it was pretty sick," said Jim.

"Yeah, it was pretty sick. We were having a lot of fights. I think the one that caused that one is I found out she was sticking the kids up in their room, because she didn't want to deal with them while I was at work. I'd come home, and the kids were still in diapers. I'd open the door and there were like torn diapers thrown all over the place."

"The children were a year and a half apart?"

"Yeah, a year apart. And these kids had been locked in this room for hours at a time and a couple of times had spread their own crap all over the walls and stuff. Here was a situation where you go from one or two violent acts to something that was just crazy. It was like *War of the Roses*. You know the movie, *War of the Roses*—it was just like that."

Again Ray was giving an idealized view of his violence. He was like a movie actor in a Hollywood black comedy. He went on to talk about how, at the time she was neglecting the children, his first wife had been abusing drugs, and that was why she hadn't wanted custody when they divorced.

"You have such an active hate for your ex-wife now," said Jim, "that it's beyond what's happened . . . it's a thing that is in you. It's one of the things that's a time bomb in you, and it's one of the things you've got to come to terms with. Also, it's a threat to your children."

"Obviously there can't be any more situations where I'm violent with her," said Ray.

"I'm not even talking about more violence between you and your ex, but about the violence that the kids sense in you. They should sense instead that there isn't a violent bone in your body, that there isn't any danger for their mom, 'cause kids can sense it."

Ray talked about how frustrated he had been with his first wife. They had been sweethearts in college where he was a football player and she was a beauty queen. At age nineteen he had felt obligated to marry her because she was pregnant. He resented that he had to work to support her and his education was interrupted. He blamed her for all his failures: she demoralized him so he couldn't concentrate in his work, she hadn't supported him in continuing his studies, and on and on.

"It worries me," said Jim, "that you talk about yourself like you're a puppet she could have stuck her hands into and done certain things with. Here you are, a talented, very intelligent man, and you're saying you didn't achieve these things and those things because you didn't get the support of a woman. I would suggest that you should achieve some of those things even without the support of a woman, and even with her interfering."

Ray needed to take responsibility not only for his violence but for his whole life.

The Fifth Session: Staying Alive

Ray's mother, Mary Jane, was invited to this session. We were approaching Christmas and hoped she would help in our effort to prevent Ray from committing suicide. We wanted to enlist her support in giving meaning to Ray's life by encouraging him to devote himself to helping his children. Ray became more helpless in the presence of his mother and began to talk about his suicidal ideas. He cried as he talked about his loneliness and despair. Jim needed to encourage him to stay alive for the sake of his children.

"I treat victims of sexual abuse," Jim said to Ray and his mother, "and I treat a lot of children. And one thing that they're always trying to figure out is 'How am I going to look at this? What kind of spin am I going to put on this whole thing?' And if you, from this point on, talk to your children like 'It's terrible. I did it. You didn't do it. But I love you and am going to take care of you and make sure you're going to be OK for the rest of your lives.' You're going to make them feel worthwhile as human beings. You're going to make them feel that no matter what happens to you, you love them and care about them, that you'll put up with anything."

"Can I tell him something to exaggerate that point?" asked Mary Jane. "I don't know if I've shared this with you, and I hope I don't cry. My brother David and I were talking about some things that had happened to us when I was less than two and he was barely five. My mother would not allow my dad to see us, and she really had no legal right to do that. So she took us out of the area where we lived and had some strange baby-sitters take care of us. She told them that my father was not allowed to come visit us, and they would lock us up in this shed when Daddy would come out to the house, if they thought there was any chance that he was going to come out. There was this little window in the shed. Now, I was too small to know what was going on, and I used to cling to my brother all the time, 'cause he was older than me, and David was big enough to step on some box and look out the window. And he remembered seeing Daddy come one time and him beating on that window, saying, 'Daddy, we're here! Daddy we're here!' Of course, Daddy couldn't hear him, the shed was too far away. And the woman said, 'I don't take care of those kids. I don't know what you're talking about.'

"And when David told me this story, his voice broke down and he started to cry. You know, David's a grown man, fifty-one years old, but he sounded like a little boy crying to me. He said, 'I just figured something out, Mary Jane. I'm still waiting for Daddy to come get me.' Don't underestimate. They'll always want their daddy to get them. Even when they're fifty-one years of age."

Ray had been listening to his mother, hypnotized. He looked more hopeful now.

"Can I have your word you're not going to hurt yourself?" asked Jim, extending his hand to shake Ray's.

"I gave you my word before. It's just that it's so difficult," said Ray, drying his tears and shaking Jim's hand.

The session continued with an optimistic discussion of interesting things that Ray could do when he came out of jail. Jim suggested that Ray could take a spiritual journey.

"I've had three weeks' vacation in ten years," said Ray.

"There are some Indian groups," said Jim, "that believe you aren't a man until you've seen certain sights and have become familiar with certain spirits. So they take these treks that are like religious journeys."

"Like rites of initiation," said Mary Jane.

"Yeah," continued Jim, "like in India, they go to all these terrific places. It's kind of like you can't be able to be a man until you've stepped outside of your situation."

The session ended in this vein, discussing pleasant, interesting things that Ray could look forward to.

The Sixth Session: Finding the Metaphor

Our goal for this session was to find the metaphor for Ray's violence. Who had programmed him for violence? Whose life was he repeating? What was there in his past? Jim invited Ray's mother again to this session in the hope of discovering what violence and abuse there had been in Ray's childhood and in previous generations in the family.

In order to produce someone like Ray, who loved and yet sexually abused his own daughter, there had to be a confusion between love and violence in previous generations of his family. We decided to start talking about Ray's confusion as to whether he loved or hated Vicky, his first wife.

"Let's say that Vicky still loves you," said Jim, "and we may disagree on this part, but for the sake of discussion, let's say you love Vicky. Because love is not a black-and-white thing. You can hate someone and love them at the same time. That's what's so darn confusing. And things get real dangerous if you can't see the mix of the two in your relationship. It's easier and more clear in your relationship with Vicky, and I think that the same thing was at work with Rosemary, although not in the same ratio. In other words, there was more time spent in violence with Vicky, but in certain ways the type of violence with Rosemary was much more damaging. We have to untangle things and make a clear difference between love and violence, because those things were confused for you. Are there any other relationships with Ray where these things might have been confused?" asked Jim, turning toward Mary Jane.

"With my husband or with my son?" asked Mary Jane.

"With your son."

"We had such an idyllic relationship with him up through the fourteenth month," said Mary Jane. All of a sudden her voice had become high pitched and childish. This was a sign that she would talk about events that she had made a great effort to forget. "He was with his father and me all the time in Texas. He was never fussed at, he was never smacked. But when we came back from Texas, I had to put him in the care of my mother during the day because I had to work until my husband found a job. He was kept in a playpen so much of the time, and I remember I called up at lunchtime once to see how he was doing, and she told me she had slapped him in his face.

"He was only sixteen or eighteen months old, so I said, 'Mom, why did you slap him in his face?' Because I can remember: I've had some vicious beatings in my lifetime. I said, 'He still has a crack in his head.' You know, to this day I'm not opposed, if necessary, to give one or two smacks to a behind or a thigh, but not to hit a child in the head. I hit him one time in the face when he was two. I sat there rocking him in my arms crying, 'I'm sorry, I'm sorry, I'm so sorry.' I swore I would never touch my children the way my parents hit me."

"Your parents hit you a lot?" asked Jim.

"Oh, God, yes. I've had eyes blackened, nose bloodied. . . . I've been beaten for a half hour at a time. Yeah, I've had a very violent upbringing. Because of that I wanted to make mine so perfect. So I sat there with this two-year-old crying and rocking him on the floor saying, 'I'm so sorry, Ray, I'm so sorry.' And I did use to rage at him a lot."

One of the more difficult problems in the therapy of sex offenders is to develop their empathy and compassion. These men can repeatedly commit sexual crimes because they have little or no feeling for the victim. Only when a man can feel empathy and compassion does he truly take responsibility for his actions toward others, because only then does he understand the consequences of his actions. Self-determination is only possible when a person takes responsibility for his behavior. So a goal of a therapy of social action is to develop the empathy and compassion that make self-determination possible.

In struggling with this problem, I thought about how our first object of empathy is our mother. As infants, our body is hardly differentiated from hers and we feel what she feels. Our mother is our first object of love, and it is only gradually that we begin to extend that love to other people, beginning with those whom our mother loves. When something goes wrong in the child's development, that love is not transferred to others. The child becomes incapable of feeling empathy and compassion. To correct this situation, the offender has to be encouraged to feel for his mother's suffering, as he must have felt in his infancy, and to recover the warm feelings of love and compassion that he must have once felt for her. Then it is possible to extend those feelings to others and to help him develop the empathy that he could not develop in childhood.

This was one of the goals for inviting Ray's mother to participate in the therapy, and that is why we welcomed the stories about how she had been abused and mistreated. Ray listened, and even when they talked later about how Mary Jane had mistreated him, there was no anger, only love for her—a good sign that he would be able to develop his compassion for others.

Mary Jane continued with the subject of when Ray was a toddler in the care of his grandmother. "It was years later that my sister said to me, 'Did you have any idea how much Mamma hated that child?' I said, 'Why do you say that?' It was all a family secret they never told me, that when Mamma would hit him, it was like having some kind of orgasmic release, that she would slap him from one end of his body to the other. I talked it over with the counselor at the hospital and she said, 'That's sexual abuse! When you get rid of that kind of energy, it's related to sex.' And I don't know if this is truth or fiction, Dr. Keim, I only know that my sister disclosed it to me years later. So it was perpetuated for about six months of his life."

I was thinking that finally I had the metaphor I had been looking for. When Ray became violent, he was not the Incredible Hulk. He was not like his father. His violence had nothing to do with manliness or with justice. When Ray became violent, he was a sexually crazed old woman. He was his grandmother. She was the monster he carried within. It was she who had programmed him for violence and sexual abuse. I felt that the image of the grandmother was sufficiently repulsive to Ray that if he truly believed that she was the monster inside him, he wouldn't engage in those behaviors again.

For a criminal to change, it is not the words of the judge or the jail sentence that matters—it is the metaphor of violence that has to change. Violence has to be given a repulsive meaning in the criminal's own life; it has to become associated with the most hated person in the criminal's own background. The criminal has to feel that he has been programmed and manipulated into violence by someone he despises. Only then will the criminal change.

Metaphors are powerful motivators. Most wars between nations and ethnic groups have been fought over ideas and symbols. Just as there has to be a metaphor for a group to become violent, so it is with the violent individual. For violence to stop, the metaphor must change. But the reframing must take place at a time when it can have the greatest impact. We would wait for the right moment. I knew that Jim would not proceed with the reframing until we planned it together.

Jim turned to Ray. "Do you remember your grandmother's violence?"

"I remember hating going over there," said Ray. "I think that in my mind, I've just forgotten a lot of it. I tried to reconcile things with her a little bit before she died, but we just didn't get along."

"Let me try to summarize," said Jim, "the different sorts of violence in your family and the confusion between love and violence." He turned to Mary Jane. "You had told me that your mother's father sexually abused your mother?" [The grandmother who abused Ray had been sexually abused by her own father.]

"All the girls in the family. It was incest. It was intercourse with those girls."

"And your father sexually abused your sister?"

"Yes, and covertly abused me and my brother."

"Sexually."

"Yes," said Mary Jane. "We were made to bend over, and he would scrub our anuses when we were big enough to do it ourselves. When we objected, he threatened to whip us."

"Your father?"

"Yes. Now he was literally drunk as a skunk when he came in and molested my sister when she was in her teens. I don't know if he realized what he was doing, but if she had not gotten away from him she might have been raped. That woman's never been right since. She's a basket case."

"Did you say that your mother abused you sexually?"

"No, my father. But what my mother did is dressed me in very seductive clothes that she made for me. I didn't like dressing that way. And I remember one time she made me walk in front of her girlfriend to show her my naked body, and I felt like an idiot. She wanted to show what was in her mind's eye a quote unquote perfect body. But I thought if I could just get my three children through without anybody bothering them, that maybe the cycle could be broken. I couldn't. Something's communicated."

"And between the two of you," said Jim, "you did much better than the previous generation, but there was still the physical violence, the raging, the loss of control."

"The loss of control," said Mary Jane. "I remember three occasions when I hit him out of control." She was contradicting herself. Previously she had said she had lost control with Ray once. "I smacked his little face when he was two and sat on the floor crying with him. When I went into the bedroom and you were screaming, 'Fire, fire, fire,' and I was going to hit you with all my might and missed and hit the bedpost. And another time when he went outside and I had said, 'Do not go outside without your shoes on.' They were doing all kinds of construction around the house, and be damned if he didn't cut his foot on a piece of glass. I was so compulsively clean then—I was like a nut, cleaning the basement like somehow I was going to put the world right by getting all the dirt out. And he comes running and screaming with his foot spewing blood everywhere, and all I could do was slap the living shit out of this kid. 'I told you not to go outside. I told you something like this was going to happen!' And there was this blood mixed in with all that water."

"Do you remember this?"

"It was a switch," said Ray. "I can remember the water in the garage. It seemed I was just bleeding to death, and this woman's hitting me with a switch."

"I remember being aggressively angry with you at that age," said Mary Jane. "The only time I remember us even touching affectionately at any time since he was a toddler was when he had broken up

with his first girlfriend, his first major heartbreak, and his father was
running around on me. Those two things coincided. And he came
and put his head on my stomach and his arms around me and cried.
But he did it so tentatively, like he was sneaking up on me, like he
thought I would push him away. In my family we never hugged, we
never touched, we never kissed. I've never been told by my mother
that she loved me. It just wasn't done. I remember before she died I
made myself go over to her and hug her and say, 'Mamma, I love
you.' I've never done anything so difficult in all my life. It felt so
abnormal, but I made myself do it. And her whole body stiffened up."

Jim talked about the importance of putting an end to violence
and sexual abuse so it wouldn't continue in the next generation.
We decided to invite Vicky, Ray's first wife, to the next session. We
knew through Shirley that Vicky might be ready to accept the invi-
tation.

Jim had been talking with Shirley on the phone from time to
time to make sure she was alright. We were concerned about her
and had offered therapy with Jim or with someone else, but she had
refused. Jim had encouraged Shirley to do everything possible to
stay in touch with the children. In one of the conversations, he suggested that Shirley call Vicky and offer to baby-sit for the children
for free. We suspected that Vicky, accustomed to the life of a single
woman, was missing her freedom. Vicky had never enjoyed staying
home, and she grabbed the opportunity. During Shirley's many visits, the two women had become best friends. They had a common
enemy: Ray. Shirley was able to continue her relationship with the
children and to see them often. She had spoken well of Jim to
Vicky, so we knew it was time to invite her.

The Seventh Session: The Monster Within

When Vicky walked into the therapy room, I was amazed at how
she resembled Ray's mother. Blonde and curvy, one could see how
she might have been a beauty queen. She sat far away from Ray, on

the opposite couch, with her coat and her purse on her lap, as if to protect herself. Ray was tense, conveying a mixture of longing and resentment toward her. Where Shirley had been quiet and withdrawn, Vicky was talkative and matter-of-fact.

"Do you have any idea what it's like to deal with a nine-year-old child who is suicidal?" Vicky asked Ray, almost shuddering with indignation.

"She was physically cutting herself, scratching her face. It was absolutely hell. 'Mom, is it really true that when people kill themselves they can't go to heaven?' And I'm in the position where the only thing I can do is say, 'Rosemary, it's true,' because I know what she's talking about and who she's talking about. 'Mommy, there's too much pain in the world. I can't take it. I don't want to live in this world because there's too much pain. Daddy did this to me because I'm ugly. Daddy didn't love me. You didn't love me, Mommy, you left me with Daddy and Daddy did this to me because I was ugly, because I was born with a hole in my face. I want to go to Jesus, Mommy, I want to go to Jesus now. I don't want to wait. Everybody tells me everything will get better when I get older. I don't want to wait until I'm older, it hurts too much right now.'

"We were scared shitless. She would come out of her room and her face would be nothing but scratches. She burned herself. It was hell. All she can see in her mind is the look you had on your face when she told on you. When Shirley confronted you about the abuse and you turned around and looked at her. That's all she can see about you."

"I just didn't want her to see me," muttered Ray, confused, as if talking to himself, his face was drawn, his expression distraught. "When I was molesting her, I just didn't want her to see me." He thought Vicky was talking about the eye contact during the abuse, while she was actually talking about when the abuse was revealed to Shirley.

"You didn't want to see her face?" asked Vicky with disgust.

"I didn't want to look at her."

"And if you were that comprehending of what you were doing, how could you still do it? If it mattered for you not to see her. . . ."

"I didn't want her to see me," interrupted Ray. "That was the biggest thing. I didn't want her to see me. It was almost like I didn't want her to know what I was doing. But obviously she knew what I was doing. . . . I don't know. . . . If she doesn't see what I'm doing maybe she won't know what I'm doing. . . ."

"There's no doubt in your mind you would have had intercourse. You would have had intercourse with her," said Vicky.

"If the abuse had gone on, yeah."

"Absolutely. You were pushing it as far as you could. What would you have done if that child had gotten pregnant with your child?"

"I don't want to think about that," said Ray, bent over, his head between his hands.

"Did none of this run through your mind? You know her hormones are starting right now."

We had been prepared to encourage Vicky to confront Ray about the abuse, but it wasn't necessary. She wanted to find out what was on his mind. Explicit conversations with the offender and family members about the abuse are essential to the therapy. Incest is possible because it is secret. As soon as it is made public, society intervenes to stop it. So the incestuous relationship has to be made public to every family member. This is the best safeguard for the prevention of sexual abuse.

"Something you may be curious about, Vicky," said Jim, "is whether Ray was sexually abused." Jim wanted to direct the conversation to Ray's childhood, thinking that he might find the right timing to reframe the metaphor of Ray's violence.

"I asked him," said Vicky. "I know his grandfather fondled him."

We didn't know about this. It seemed to me that in every session new incidents of abuse were revealed.

"I had my clothes on," said Ray, "what he actually did is . . . I was getting out of the back of the station wagon. . . . I was about eight or ten years old, and he ran his hand along the backside of my thigh and grabbed my balls, basically."

"And how do you know that was the only time?" asked Vicky. "Just because you can remember it?"

"It's the only time I can remember."

"It's also a question," said Jim, "of whether your grand-mother. . . ."

"Physically, viciously abused him," interrupted Vicky, "and can I say something?"

"Yeah," said Jim.

"Your mother said something to me that threw me on my ass. Her sister had told her that the most eerie thing about the abuse that your grandmother inflicted on you was that she enjoyed it. She was smiling. I just about hit the floor. You know why? Because when you abused me you were smiling. That was the most haunting thing about what you did." Vicky was seeing the connection between the grandmother's abuse and Ray's violence. She knew that Ray carried his grandmother inside him.

"There's something I wanted to tell you about our abuse," said Ray. "I got into it a little when we were seeing the other therapist in Virginia, but I never was honest with her about what really hap-pened." Ray turned to Jim. "I was going through these times when I would wake up in the middle of the night hallucinating that Vicky was this demon beside me, and I'd be staring at her and think I could just will this thing away. It was weird, I went through this period of about a year where I'd see her and somehow she was changing herself into a . . . I can't really explain it. Did you ever see *The Exorcist?* Well, I went home the night I saw *The Exorcist* and felt this cold presence in the room. I might have been psyching myself out, but I used to get this cold feeling, like it was a battle of wills. At the time I was really involved in this religious thing, and it seemed like there was this other force, pulling me . . . that I was fighting this other force all the time. At this time this demon was coming through her."

"Was it just when you'd wake up in the middle of the night?" asked Jim.

"I somehow developed this thing," said Ray, "where I could go to sleep right in the middle of her arguing with me. I'd go to sleep, just fade away, and I remember she would poke me: 'Wake up! Why are you going to sleep on me?' Then it was like waking someone out of a trance and I was crazy. I was ready to tear somebody's head off. To me this was significant because it was almost like I was on a spiritual high. . . . I felt like I was on some mission from God . . . , and I remember the biggest thing in my life was to be ordained a priest in this church I was going to. But the closer I got to that, this other half was pulling me apart . . . the violent part that would hurt her."

"A real presence in your early childhood," said Jim, "was a grandmother who was losing control in a bizarre sexual way, and. . . ."

"I used to see you smiling at me that way," interrupted Ray, talking to Vicky, "like my grandmother used to smile at me. . . . My mother was able to do it too. . . . It was kind of like an evil smile." Ray seemed to be looking inside himself. "I can remember it now . . . yeah. My grandmother used to just about knock my head clear off my shoulders. She would sit there and smile at me about it. I remember it would be just like 'Shut up Ray!' and then just 'Bap!'" He made the exact same gesture with the back of his hand that he had made when describing the first time he had hit Vicky.

Vicky burst out crying. "You're scaring me!" There was a silence as she sobbed.

"You OK?" asked Ray and then continued to talk as if he was back in time. "I just remembered that. Such a long time . . . I don't even remember how old I was when that happened."

This was one of those unusual moments in therapy when someone recovers a lost traumatic memory from childhood. Even though

Mary Jane had told Ray about the grandmother's abuse, this was the first time that he was able to remember it. Now was the right timing to reframe the violence inside Ray. From behind the one-way mirror, I called Jim on the phone and told him to go ahead with the reframing we had planned.

"As terrible as this is," said Jim, "this is the kind of crazy cocktail that results in sexual abuse. You have adults who are completely inappropriate at times, losing control in a way that has sexual overtones."

Ray spoke as if still in a dream. "She would start with 'Hello, little Ray! Hee! Hee!' And it was a kind of laugh that was like 'I hate you!'"

"And there's this confusion that you have to get straight between love and violence," said Jim. "And the way to get straight is to understand the boundary between the two, despite the fact that they were mixed when you were a child. You had that kind of background. You hadn't worked out the boundary between love, sex, and violence."

"I never remembered that until just now." Ray seemed shocked.

"It's a sign that you're starting to put these things in the right categories," said Jim. "You have to know how to file these memories. You have to know how to look at the past and say, 'These are some terrible things that happened to me, and this is what was wrong with them.'"

"Just as Rosemary will have to do," said Vicky.

"Yes," said Jim.

"Just like I handled it," said Vicky, referring to Ray's violence against her.

"Until you have filed them properly," said Jim, "they will come out in a way that doesn't make sense with the rest of you. In other words, if you haven't clarified what this was about, it's going to influence you. But it doesn't have to."

"That's why I went off like that the first time you ever hit me," said Ray.

"You mentioned your fight with a roommate . . . ," said Jim.

Ray interrupted, "I look back now and see . . . but at the time I was always proud of it. I was always proud that I had this nuclear bomb in my arsenal when I needed it. If someone pushed me, I was going to knock their head clean off, because I was that crazy!"

"See," said Jim, "you have to be at the point where that's not a tool anymore. Your grandmother used it like a tool, and you were like in a time warp when you used it in your relationship. Did he give an accurate description of his violence, Vicky?"

"Yes."

"It's like you had a button inside of you, and if you pushed it you were in the grandmother mode, and any violence was possible."

"I saw your father," said Vicky, "the physical things he did to your sister Rose, coming flying out of the room with a piece of wood sticking out of her hand. And he almost broke Sally's arm. Your mother comes downstairs with a bloody lip. He almost came after me, until you put him against the wall!"

It seemed to me that every time we were about to reach closure on the issue of violence, new incidents were remembered.

"He wasn't coming after you," said Ray.

"Don't tell me," said Vicky, "he had the same look in his face that you had! He also threw you against the bedroom wall when you were three and gave you a bloody nose. Your mother took me aside to her bedroom and told me you were going to be a wife beater, Ray, and I didn't believe her."

"When you thought of all this before," said Jim, "you thought of a powerful masculine side coming out of you. But the real face of it was a sexually abusing, crazed grandmother. That's the force. So when you get that out-of-control feeling, Ray, in that grandmother mode, you have to feel the same way as when you think of what you did to your daughter: shocked. There has to be repugnance. That's what's connected with being out of control. You have to put the face on it that goes with it."

At the end of this session, I breathed a sigh of relief. The main work of the therapy was done. I didn't think that Ray would be abusive or violent again. The next stage (while waiting until we could have an apology session with Rosemary) would be the slow process of pulling Ray out of his isolation and loneliness.

The Next Twenty Sessions: Fighting Loneliness

Shirley, Ray's second wife, waited until the day Ray came out of jail to leave him. When she left Ray's home and filed for divorce, he was devastated and became dangerously suicidal. In jail he had idealized Shirley and felt that no other woman would ever want to be with him. Following my suggestions, Jim told him that he needed to accept the fact that Shirley had not been good for him. Even though Ray had total responsibility for the abuse of Rosemary, the reality was that it had happened while he was living with Shirley. The truth was that Shirley did not bring out the best in him. Jim reassured him that eventually he would find a woman that would be good for him.

During the first couple of months after coming out of jail, Ray was so lonely that Jim, who worked on weekends, would have him come to the office and sit in the waiting room just so he could have some human contact. Ray was a talented artist, and he painted watercolors while he waited to have a few words with Jim between other people's sessions.

During this time, Ray's sisters came to visit him, participated in a couple of sessions, and offered their support and friendship.

The Apology Session

It took nine months from the beginning of the therapy for Rosemary's therapist to give permission for a session with Ray. He finally conceded because after Rosemary received Ray's letter of apology, all she would talk about in the sessions was that she needed to see her father. So finally the therapist told Jim that there could be a session but it had to be in his office, in his presence. So Jim went with Ray to this therapist's office where Vicky and Rosemary were present.

As soon as Ray walked into the room and saw Rosemary, he fell on his knees crying. His words of sorrow and repentance were deeply moving and sincere. When he finished, Rosemary said, "You took a knife out of my heart."

Vicky was so moved by Ray's apology and by Rosemary's response that she went to court and asked the judge to give Ray supervised visitation with the children, offering that she and Ray's mother could be the supervisors. So nine months after the beginning of the therapy, Ray was seeing his children regularly on weekends, taking them to interesting places in Washington, and actively working to heal the relationship.

The End of Therapy

The therapy went on for two years, with sessions every two weeks during the last nine months. It ended by mutual agreement when Ray was no longer suicidal, had begun to date and enjoy a few friends, continued to work, and saw his children regularly under the supervision of his mother. He was very grateful for the therapy and even wrote a letter to a newspaper about the importance of giving the right therapy to sex offenders. He felt the therapy had given him the power of self-determination, which in the past he had never felt he had.

After the therapy ended, Ray fell in love with a woman but later discovered that her first husband had molested their daughter. He was shocked that the woman had picked him before knowing what he had done, and he broke off that relationship. One year later he was seriously involved with another woman.

Vicky moved with the children to another state to be closer

to her parents who helped her get a good job and also took a great interest in the children. Ray, however, is not their favorite person, and they don't make it easy for him to visit with the children. He continues to see them under the supervision of his mother, but now he or the children have to travel for the visits. I am pleased to report that the children are now close to Vicky's family, which does not have a history of incest and violence.

Steps in the Therapy of Adult Sex Offenders

A s we have seen in the two cases presented so far, it's best to plan the therapy of sex offenders as a series of steps to be followed in an organized way. This way of doing therapy is useful to control the therapist's anxiety in working with these sad, difficult problems. There is always an attainable goal: to carry out one step and then move to the next one. Sometimes several steps can be accomplished in one session. Sometimes the therapy moves slowly. But there are always clear goals.

Here I will present the steps for the therapy of an adult who may have committed a crime against his own child, a stepchild, niece, nephew, grandchild, or other relative. The steps are described in terms of how to proceed when the offender is a father. Later, I will address other circumstances.

In the United States, the offender is always court-ordered to therapy, or there is some other kind of involvement with the criminal justice system, since any professional person who suspects an adult of committing a sexual crime must report him to the authorities. In most cases when the therapy starts, the offender is already involved with the legal system, but, if the abuse is discovered during the therapy, the therapist must report the offender to the police and the Department of Social Services. So either before the trial or after, the offender stands to gain by cooperating with the therapist, whose opinion of the collaboration with the therapy and amenability to change is usually requested by the court. This leverage is important since, at the beginning of the therapy, many offenders are not repentant and only participate because of a court order.

Step 1: Exposing the Offense

The offender usually has been removed from the family at the beginning of therapy and is forbidden by the court to have any contact with the victim or his other children. So the therapist begins by either meeting with the offender alone and gradually bringing in other members of the family until permission is obtained to have an apology session with the victim; or the therapist meets with the victim and the family and, if possible, separately with the offender, until it's possible to bring them together.

Usually the judge will grant permission if the therapist suggests that there will be court personnel or other therapists present and that victim and victimizer will never be alone together. Even if the offender is in jail, family sessions can be arranged with special permission.

Sometimes the victim and the family don't want to see the offender, so it's important to convince them that nothing will be asked of them except their presence for a few minutes. They don't have to talk to him or even look at him. All they have to do is hear what he has to say. They don't have to answer. It's very rare for the family or the victim to object when the therapist explains clearly that this is for one session and for the purpose of a very specific communication from the offender.

After establishing some rapport with the offender and the family, inquiring about their life, their work, and so forth, the first step is to obtain clear and concrete information on the sex offense. What exactly did the father do to the child? Where did he do it? How often? Who knew or suspected it? The therapist needs to talk to the offender and also involve relatives as early as possible. Ideally, in the first interview, the whole family is gathered: mother, father, all the children, grandparents, and other relatives. The therapist goes around the circle asking each one about everything they knew or suspected about the offense.

It's very important to use explicit language. The therapist must feel comfortable using words such as penis and vagina and must use language that assigns responsibility. For example, instead of asking, "What happened?" the question should be something like "Tell me what sexual acts you forced her to perform," or "Tell me what sexual things you did to her."

This isn't something that "happened." This is something that someone did to somebody else. The choice of words is very important because this is a therapy of assigning responsibility, which has to be clear from the very beginning. Most of all, the victim has to hear that the offender has all the responsibility for the crime, that she or he didn't bring this upon themselves.

The therapist needs to ask the offender questions skillfully, showing such respect, sympathy, and understanding that the offender will be able to relate to the therapist precisely what he did to the victim. Then the therapist can point out that those actions were solely the responsibility of the offender. Neither the victim nor anyone else is to blame. The therapy cannot proceed until the offender has taken responsibility.

A very important principle of this therapy is that there should be no pressure on the victim. Any pressure on the victim can be experienced as taking away responsibility from the offender. A therapy of social action is based on moral concepts where victim and victimizer are not equal and don't share responsibility. Even being asked a question can be experienced as pressure and humiliation by someone who has been sexually abused. So when the therapist goes around the circle asking each one what they know about the offense, it's very important not to ask anything directly of the victim. The art for the therapist is to indicate that the victim can speak if she wants to but that she doesn't have to.

This first step is important because it's usually the first time that the family sits together and talks about the abuse. It's crucial that everyone should know about it because incest is possible because it is secret. As soon as it is made public, society intervenes to stop it. So it needs to be made public within the family. A basic principle of the therapy is that there should be no more secrets in the family. A secret can lead to another inappropriate coalition and to another situation of incest. Perhaps in families without incest, people can have secrets from each other, but once incest has been committed, there can be no more secrets.

It's very important to include elders in the family (parents of the offender, or grandparents, uncles, aunts, or any other older relatives) at the beginning of the therapy. This will make the therapy easier for the therapist. If the relatives cannot come to the first session, the therapist has to go through this first step of the account of the sex offense again when the relatives are present. In fact, all the steps for which the relatives were not present should be repeated or summarized for their benefit. It's always possible to bring relatives in for at least one session, even if they have to cover long distances, if the therapist conveys how important their participation is to help the child and to prevent further abuse. If they come from far away, the therapist can have long sessions, covering many steps in one or two days. Grandparents, even if they have not been good parents, usually welcome the opportunity to do something for their grandchildren, perhaps as a way of compensating for their behavior as parents. Sometimes the offender will say that he is estranged from his family, or the wife might say that she doesn't like them. This is all the more reason to bring them in and try to restore those relationships. The therapist must remember that the goal is to reorganize the tribe so that the elders can protect the children and the therapist is no longer needed.

The presence of the relatives is particularly important because typically the offender will show hostility and defiance toward the therapist, his wife, and his children. But a man who has sex with a child is an extremely immature person. He will often behave like a child as soon as he is in the presence of his mother or father or other older relatives. His defiance and hostility will disappear, and it will be much easier to conduct the therapy.

Sometimes families would prefer not to have young children present in the session when the offense is discussed. This should only be allowed if the therapist feels that there is no threat of abuse to the younger children. Otherwise it's best to have them present so that the children are not anxious and mystified about the family problem. Secrecy does not help or protect them. When there are young children, it's necessary to provide them with dolls, paper, and crayons, so they can express themselves.

Sometimes the father or the family will state or imply that the victim provoked the abuse. In fact, sometimes the father appears thought disordered in believing that even a very young child would have wanted the sexual act. The therapist might think that the father is psychotic, but during the course of the therapy, as various steps are accomplished, this idea will dissolve. It must be made very clear to everyone that the court and the therapist don't accept any idea of provocation. Sometimes when the victim is an adolescent girl, she might say that she actually did provoke her father and she remembers enjoying the sexual relationship. The therapist must say that this is all the more blame to the father, since a father should protect his daughter from such feelings instead of encouraging them.

Step 2: Confronting Why It Was Wrong

After getting an account of the sex offense, the therapist needs to ask the father why what he did to the child was wrong. The father might answer that it was against the law, against the religion, that it interfered with the child's normal development, or that it was violent. The therapist can then ask, Why is it against the law? Why shouldn't an adult—a father—have sex with a child? How is it violent, and why is violence wrong? How does sex with an adult interfere in the child's normal development?

We pursue these questions until the offender admits to the element of force and coercion that he perpetrated on the child and to the brutality, exploitation, and manipulation involved. Then the therapist asks the offender how he thinks the child must have felt and pursues the question until the father can empathize with the fear, despair, and betrayal that the child must have experienced and how these feelings are related to current problems and symptoms presented by the child.

The level of confrontation by the therapist in this conversation depends on the father's level of denial and on how suicidal he might be. The father needs to take responsibility for his actions and fully understand the horror of what he did, yet the therapist doesn't want him to kill himself. The art of the therapy consists in knowing when to stop confronting and move to the next step, so the man can see that there is some hope for healing.

The therapist then says that even though the sexual crime was wrong for all those important issues that have just been discussed, it was wrong for one other, most important reason. She then asks the other adults in the room to help the father understand what this is. They might add more information about the child's fears and symptoms, or they may talk about what it must feel like to a child to be used as an object to satisfy brutal sexual impulses that the child cannot even understand, and how this has affected the child's self-esteem and sense of identity. The therapist agrees with all this.

Step 3: Explaining Spiritual Pain

Then the therapist says that it was wrong for one most important reason, and that is that it caused a spiritual pain in the child. Sexuality and spirituality are related in human beings, so a sexual attack is an attack on the spirit of the person, specially when the attack comes from someone that the child loves, trusts, and on whom the child is dependent—the father.

Society recognizes this pain and punishes sexual crimes more severely than other crimes. If the therapist is uncomfortable with using the word *spiritual*, he or she can say that the abuse caused "a pain in the heart" of the child. Since, in our culture, the heart is the center of spirituality, everyone will understand what the therapist is talking about.

Of more than 100 families of sexual abuse that have been seen at my institute, not one objected to this concept of spiritual pain. In fact, the families are relieved because the therapist has given a name to a pain that they experienced and that they knew was different. When the therapist has acknowledged that pain, the family feels understood and it's easier to conduct the therapy.

The spirit is the center of human values such as beauty, goodness, love, truth, compassion, and honesty. These values constitute the essence of consciousness, of what is human. When wounded, we hurt at the core of our being. But this pain also offers the possibility of transcendence.

The experience of coming into contact with this pain can be overwhelming to a therapist, particularly to one who has not experienced the pain himself. The therapist needs to find strength and hopefulness in herself in order to give hope and strength to the victim and the family. I find it useful to keep a constant picture in my mind of the lives of people who have suffered great spiritual pain and not only overcame the pain but became a source of universal inspiration.

One such person is Maya Angelou, who was raped at age seven by a man who was later killed by her family. She became mute and did not speak for five years.

"Now to show you how out of evil there can come good," she says, "in those five years I read every book in the Black school library; I read all the books I could get from the White school library; I memorized James Weldon Johnson, Paul Laurence Dunbar, Countee Cullen, and Langston Hughes; I memorized Shakespeare, whole plays, 50 sonnets; I memorized Edgar Allan Poe, all the poetry—never having heard it, I memorized it. I had Longfellow, I had Guy de Maupassant, I had Balzac, Rudyard Kipling. . . . When I decided to speak, I had a lot to say, and many ways in which to say what I had to say. . . ."

She says about her experience of sexual abuse that it was "a dire kind of evil, because rape on the body of a young person more often than not introduces cynicism, and there is nothing quite so tragic as a young cynic, because it means the person has gone from knowing nothing to believing nothing. In my case I was saved in that muteness. And out of this evil I was able to draw from human thought, human disappointments and triumphs, enough to triumph myself."

Out of her silence, Maya Angelou developed the strength to recover her inner self, her spirit, and then to transcend herself connecting, through her poetry, to the universal. She did it alone. Not everyone can speak to a universal connection with humanity like she does, but everyone can recover from a wounded spirit. It is our job as therapists to assist in the healing of the spirit.

In the words of Thich Nhat Hanh, the Vietnamese monk, "A human being is like a television set with millions of channels. . . . If we turn sorrow on, we are sorrow. If we turn a smile on, we really are the smile. We cannot let just one channel dominate us. We have the seed of everything in us, and we have to seize the situation in our hand, to recover our own sovereignty."

In order to understand good, we must understand evil. Most therapists feel that they can understand the pain of the victim. But I believe that in order to truly understand spiritual pain, one must understand the pain of the victimizer. To be a therapist in the true sense of the word, we must be able not only to help the victim heal but also to pull the offender out of his spiritual despair. Because not only the pain of the victim but also the pain of the offender is a part of us all, a part of the universal human drama. To change the victimizer, we must have the courage to come into contact with the darkest side of human nature.

Rabbi Shelomo once said, "If you want to raise a man from mud and filth, do not think it is enough to keep standing on top and reaching down to him a helping hand. You must go all the way down yourself, down into mud and filth. Then take hold of him with strong hands and pull him and yourself out into the light."

Step 4: Revealing Other Victims and Victimizers

Step 4 usually happens spontaneously. After talking about spiritual pain, the family reveals that there are other victims and victimizers in the family. The wife or the mother may have been molested as a child and may talk about how they wanted to protect the victim so she or he wouldn't suffer like they did. The therapist can point out that research shows that sexual abuse happens in several generations in the family and that the goal of the therapy is that no more children be victimized in this or future generations. That's why the participation of everyone is necessary.

The offender may have been sexually abused himself. If so, the therapist needs to say that having suffered victimization is no excuse to inflict it on someone else. On the contrary, precisely because the offender knows the spiritual pain of the victim, he should never inflict this pain on somebody else.

Sometimes there are so many victims and victimizers in the family, the therapist may be tempted to change focus to the problems of other family members. But, as a general rule, it's better to stay focused on the presenting problem, and then go through the steps again later for another family member. Sometimes, on the other hand, the therapist discovers ongoing abuse of another child and must report it and focus the therapy on this child also. In some cases, several children have been abused by various adults, and the therapist needs to go through the steps for all of them at the same time, as a group.

Step 5: Acknowledging the
Spiritual Pain of the Offender

In this step, the therapist acknowledges that the attack on the child also caused a spiritual pain in the offender because it is so terrible to do something like this to a child, particularly a child whom one loves and whom one should have wanted to protect. So the therapist acknowledges the spiritual pain of the offender for having committed the crime.

Step 6: Recognizing the Mother's Pain

The therapist must tell the family that the attack on the child was an attack on the mother because this is the child that she loves and whom she would have wanted to protect. So, in victimizing the child, the offender was victimizing the mother. He was also attacking the grandparents and the other children in the family, since this is the child whom they love.

So the therapist recognizes that the attack on the child is metaphorically an attack on the whole family, particularly on the child's mother. In a therapy of social action, violence is not an impulse or an isolated action; it is a social intervention that impinges on everyone's life.

Step 7: Apologizing on the Knees

The therapist asks the offender to get on the floor, on his knees in front of the victim, and express sorrow and repentance for what he did, saying that he takes full responsibility, that the victim is not to blame, and that he will never do anything like this again to another human being. The family and the therapist will judge whether or not he's sincere. There must be family members present during the apology because it has to be public and involve a public humiliation.

Sometimes the offender objects to getting on his knees because it's humiliating. The therapist has to say that precisely because it's humiliating he has to get on his knees, that what he did to the victim was very humiliating and caused spiritual pain, and therefore, in apologizing, the offender has to take the posture of spiritual humility.

Sometimes the offender will say something like "Please forgive me." The therapist needs to interrupt and say that the offender is in no position to ask anything of the victim and "Forgive me" is a request. This is not about forgiveness—it's about repentance and sorrow.

Usually, after the therapist has talked about the spiritual pain, the father will get on his knees and apologize sincerely and spontaneously, often crying. Then the therapist can ask the family whether they feel the apology was sincere, and, if not, he will have to apologize over and over again, in this and in other sessions until everyone is convinced of his sincerity. It's easy to recognize sincerity through choice of words, tone of voice, body posture, and what the offender chooses to say as an apology. It's extremely rare that the whole family and the therapist are not in agreement about whether the apology is heartfelt.

When the father refuses to apologize, it may be because there is an attorney telling him to deny everything. One should try to influence the lawyer to recognize the importance of admitting the truth so the offender will not repeat the crime, but the attempt generally fails. In these cases one should bring to bear the pressure of all the rest of the family, bringing in relatives to the sessions who will talk about what they saw, what they knew or suspected, until there is so much pressure on the offender that he will admit to his actions.

Sometimes even this attempt fails. Yet the apology on the knees is essential to the therapy. So what the therapist can do is say to the father that perhaps the family will never really know what exactly he did or whether he actually did what he was accused of doing. Yet he has to admit that he is responsible for having such bad communication with his child that the child would have construed whatever he did as sexual abuse. So, even if for nothing else, he has to get on the floor in front of the child and apologize for the bad relationship and the poor communication with the child. The point is that the therapist must find a way of getting the father to apologize on his knees even if he refuses to take responsibility for the sexual abuse.

In teaching these steps, I have often been asked why I advocate specifically the apology on the knees. Apologizing on one's knees is a universal symbol of humbling oneself, of humility, repentance, and respect. Why not some other act? I was looking for an act that expressed, at least to a certain extent, the drama and seriousness of the situation. It also diminishes the father in size, puts him down in relation to the child and to the rest of the family. It is from this position that he will have to start over and try to repair the damage he has caused. I couldn't think of any other act that expressed all this and was legal and ethical in the context of a therapy session.

This apology on the knees is the first step in getting past the crime he committed. Most important, this step is essential for the mental health of the victim. She has to hear from the offender, in the presence of the family, that she is not to blame, that he takes full responsibility for the crime, and that he is repentant and will not hurt her again. The therapist may also want the offender to apologize on his knees to the other family members who most love the child he hurt, such as the mother, the brothers and sisters, and the grandparents.

During the apology, the offender needs to express that he understands the spiritual pain that he caused in the child. The child is not expected to respond in any way. If there is a delay in arranging for an apology session with the child because of a court order, a letter of apology must be written by the father, approved by the therapist, and sent to the child at the beginning of the therapy. Later, when the therapist can arrange it, the apology session can take place.

Also, the offender needs to express his repentance and sorrow, not just to the child but to at least one significant relative who loves the child and would have wanted to protect her or him. This relative may be the mother, the grandparents, the stepmother, uncles and aunts, and so forth. The apology needs to be sincere, and there can be no request for forgiveness. The therapy is about repentance and reparation, not about forgiveness.

Step 8: Asking for the Mother's Apology

After the father's apology, the therapist needs to ask the mother of the victim to get on the floor on her knees in front of the child and express her sorrow and repentance for not having protected her from the father. This step is almost as important as the father's apology for the following reasons.

When a child is sexually molested by an adult, especially by one as significant as the father, there is a seduction, almost an hypnotic procedure, that is involved. The father makes the child feel, through a kind of brainwashing, that the child wanted the sexual relationship, that she provoked it or was somehow to blame. So the child can remain, for years or even the rest of her life, believing that she was to blame. She will carry a shame that will undermine her identity and interfere with her life in many devastating ways. The mother's sincere apology on her knees for not having protected the child indicates that the child was not expected to protect herself, that adults should protect children, and that she was not to blame.

There is another reason why the apology of the mother is important. When the abuser of a child is the father, he is usually very fearful of being discovered. So he threatens the child and swears her to secrecy for fear that if she reveals the secret, terrible things will happen to her, and perhaps not only to her but also to the mother and the other children as well.

Sometimes the mother refuses to apologize, saying that there was no way she could have known or protected the child, that the father was too conniving and deceitful, and that, in fact, she resents the therapist's request because it implies that she was somehow involved or responsible for the incest. But the therapist must insist, arguing that it is a mother's duty to protect a child even when it's very difficult. If nothing else, the mother should get on her knees and apologize to the child for not having had good enough communication with her that the child would have told her what she was going through.

This is so important because it's the first step in the process of restoring the relationship between mother and child. One of the saddest aspects of incest is how the mother may become estranged from the child. Because of the father's threats, the child is so afraid of revealing the secret that she often withdraws from the mother for fear that if she talks with her, the secret will accidentally come out. In these cases, the mother notices that the child withdraws from her and assumes that the child doesn't like her. So eventually she responds to the child's withdrawal by distancing herself. Soon the child has lost not only a father but also a mother.

I believe that a similar mechanism is involved in the learning difficulties that are prevalent in victims of incest. When the child is at school, so much mental energy is expended in not revealing the secret that the child cannot pay attention to what is being taught. She has to concentrate on repressing the secret. Only when the secret is lifted and the child is convinced that she was not to blame can she begin to recover her mental energy and intelligence.

When there are grandparents, they should also kneel before the child and apologize for not having protected her, or at least for not having enough good communication with her that the child would have come to them, even if she couldn't go to the mother. The siblings should also apologize, not because they could have necessarily helped or protected the child but because they need to say something in terms of how sorry they are that this happened to their sister. Siblings often feel guilty, thinking that they were spared because she was attacked, and the therapist needs to let them express their sorrow and their solidarity with their sister. The whole family circle of the victim must be involved, giving recognition to the fact that the attack on the victim was an attack on an entire social system.

Step 9: Discussing Consequences of Possible Future Crimes

The therapist needs to discuss with the adults in the family what the consequences would be if the father were to molest this or any other child again. Grandparents, uncles, aunts, and any adults or elders from the extended family or the community should be included in this discussion. The goal is to make it clear to the offender that should there be even a suspicion that he is involved in anything similar, he will be expelled from the family and from the community. The family needs to exert as much pressure as possible on the offender. The relatives can make it clear that if the offense is repeated, they will exert all their influence to ensure that the father suffers the maximum legal consequences and loses his position in the community and at work. When the father is already in jail, the relatives can make it clear that they will allow him to have a part in family life in the future only if his behavior is faultless.

Step 10: Finding a Protector

The therapist needs to find out from the family who is the most responsible, trusted, caring person in the extended family so that this person can be set up to be a special protector for the victim. Rarely can the mother be the protector at first. She is usually too weak to protect the child. Ultimately, as a result of the therapy she should be sufficiently strong, but at this point to ask her to be the special protector is putting too much pressure on her and is not realistic. It's best to look for a strong uncle, or a grandmother or two, to protect the child. One tries to find someone who is somewhat scary to the father and who feels passionately about protecting the child against abuse—someone who can say, "If you touch that child again, I'll break your head!"

Once a protector is identified, the therapist invites him or her to a session and explains that the child needs someone special to look over her and to give some guidance and comfort. That is, the protector will be like a godparent to the child. He or she must be alert for signs that the child is being abused again. The therapist explains that the signs are the same as for other child problems: appearing withdrawn, unhappy, doing poorly in school, physical complaints, and so forth. If these signs are present, the protector should contact the therapist right away.

The therapist explains that the reason the role of the protector is so important is that research shows that children who have been molested tend to be molested over and over again, or they frequently become victimizers themselves, molesting other children.

I have a theory about why this happens, but I don't have any data to prove or disprove it. I believe that because of the spiritual pain associated with sexual abuse, the child becomes obsessed with the mind of the father, thinking thoughts such as "What was he thinking while he was abusing me?" "Did he love me or hate me?" "Was the purpose to hurt me?" "How could he have done that to me? Why me?"

Since the child cannot answer these questions, eventually he or she thinks, "If I do the same thing to somebody else, then I will be in his place and understand his mind—I will know what he was thinking." Or the child thinks, "If I'm victimized again, by someone else, then this time I'll understand and I'll know what he was thinking."

It's very important to dissociate the child from this obsessing with the mind of the offender, which is similar to the experience of some victims of torture, who stay obsessed for long periods of time with their torturer. I like to say to the child that it's pointless to think about what was in the mind of the offender. While he was committing the abuse, he was just stupid and evil. That doesn't mean that he will always be stupid and evil, but at the time he was. He had no feelings, no motivations; he wasn't thinking anything. In order to be able to say this with conviction, I have used as an inspiration Hanna Arendt's thoughts about the banality of evil in her book *Eichmann in Jerusalem*.

I truly believe that certain behaviors can only be called evil. No other explanation applies. That is why I'm reluctant to give a child molester any other diagnosis. To say, for example, that he is schizophrenic or alcoholic is to insult all the good schizophrenics and the good alcoholics who never hurt anyone.

Step 11: Deciding on Reparation

The family has to decide on something the father can do as reparation to the victim. It is best if it's something that involves quite a bit of sacrifice and takes a considerable period of time. The offender has to envision that he will do reparation to the child perhaps for the rest of his life. He needs to do this in order to overcome his pain. The child needs it in order to heal.

The grandparents, for example, can make sure that the father will open a special account in the name of the victim where he will deposit money every month toward her college education. It's best if the reparation is in relation to a worthwhile cause, such as education. The family certainly has to ensure that the offender will work to support his children, not just the victim, and to ensure their well-being and safety.

Step 12: Focusing on Sexuality

As the therapy progresses, we need to focus on helping the offender develop a normal life. Decisions must be made as to how and with whom he will live. If the father was married or living with the child's mother or stepmother, will they continue to be together? Whether or not they separate, several sessions need to be devoted to the couple's relationship. If they will be together, their sex life needs to be addressed and a number of sessions devoted to sex therapy.

Whether or not the father will stay in the marriage, the therapist needs to focus specifically on his inappropriate sexual impulses and fantasies. This is a therapy of repression. We are not interested in exploring the man's fantasies. We already know that they are wrong. To explore them might encourage their development. We need to do the opposite and discourage all but the most appropriate sexual fantasies.

The therapist can explain to the father that most people are capable of all kinds of sexual pleasure. Yet most of us, at an early age, make the decision that there are certain sexual activities in which we will never engage. Not only that, but we never have those fantasies.

The offender did not make that decision early on, but he has to make it now. He must make the decision that he will never engage again in any sexual behaviors with children, and he will never allow himself the fantasy of any sexual behavior with children. Normal men, who have not molested a child, can allow themselves all kinds of sexual fantasies. But once a man has committed a sexual crime, he cannot allow himself any sexual fantasies except those involving normal sex with a consenting adult.

The therapist has to plan with the offender what he will do if the wrong sexual impulse strikes. First, he must leave the place, wherever he is, immediately. He must leave running, not walking. He has to go immediately to a phone and contact the therapist. (There always needs to be a therapist on call for emergencies in these cases, since it's possible to talk the offender out of committing another crime.) In some cases, he must run to his mother's house and tell her about his impulses. Or he can find a friend and go eat a hamburger at McDonald's. Or he can go to church and pray. All these alternatives need to be discussed, so the offender has specific ideas about what he can do instead of giving in to the sexual impulse. It must be clear that he cannot only never touch a child again; he cannot even look at a child for a sustained period of time. When masturbating he can only look at pictures of adults, not children.

The therapist also needs to discuss sexuality with the victim in individual sessions. It's best to take the approach, individually and in the presence of the family, that, no matter what the trauma, it can be overcome and the child will be able to have a happy, normal life. There are different ways of emphasizing hopefulness.

The therapist can talk about the good things that were happening in the child's life even as the abuse was going on. Perhaps the child had good friends, enjoyed a sport, or had a favorite teacher. It can also be emphasized that the abuse may seem so important now because the child is young, but as the years go by, other things that are good and much more important will happen. The child will graduate from school and go to college, fall in love and get married, perhaps become a doctor or a lawyer, give birth to a first child, and so on. The abuse will seem less and less important in the context of all the other things that will happen in the child's life.

The therapist can also ask the child to figure out approximately how many hours or minutes were actually involved in the abuse, and then ask what the child thinks her life expectancy could be. So if, for example, there were five hours of abuse, and the life expectancy is eighty years, in eighty years there are 700,800 hours, which means that only five out of 700,800 hours of the child's life were involved in being abused. In these ways the therapist struggles to prevent the child from defining herself as a victim.

The therapist needs to convey clearly to the child and the family that the victimization is a very small part of the child's life and will not affect the child's self-determination. Otherwise, the therapist's own fears and pessimism may become a self-fulfilling prophecy, and the sexual life of the victim may be affected for many years. When the child believes that she is not to blame, that the family does not blame her, and that the offender is truly repentant, she will be able to have good sexual experiences in the future. That is why family therapy is so important—as long as the child carries the secret, she carries the shame; and as long as her innocence is not revindicated by the family, she carries the guilt that can affect her sexuality and relationships for years to come.

When the family has not gone through these steps, the victim may become "promiscuous" (which in fact means that she will be victimized over and over again) or may become an offender, in an attempt to come to terms with what happened to her as a child. By the end of the therapy the therapist must be certain that the victim feels that, even though something bad happened to her, it will not affect the rest of her life and it has not limited her opportunities or her choices.

Step 13: Finding a New Metaphor

Sexual abuse often comes together with other forms of violence. The therapist needs to inquire about other violent acts committed by the offender, about violence inflicted on him as a child, and about other violence in the family. The goal of the therapy is not only to stop sex abuse but also to end other forms of violence. That is, if the sex abuse is to stop, the violence must also stop.

The therapist needs to talk with the offender and with relatives to discover if and how the offender was abused as a child. This is not in any way to justify the offender's actions—many abused children never abuse anyone. It is to discover the origin of the confusion between love and violence that makes it possible for the offender to love and abuse someone he loves. The therapist must assume that in the offender's childhood there was someone that was supposed to love and protect him but abused him instead. Then the therapist can introduce the idea that the offender carries this person inside of him, this "alien" who has programmed him for violence.

Most offenders think of violence as something "macho," heroic, idealized in some way. To counter this metaphor, the therapist has to find a metaphor for violence that is totally despicable to the offender. The offender must understand that violence was implanted in him by the person who most hurt him in his childhood, by the one he most despises. For a criminal to change, violence must become associated with a significant other who is alien to him, so that he can feel that when he is violent, he is just a puppet programmed by someone he hates.

Once the therapist understands how the offender has been programmed and by whom, then the therapist has a metaphor for the offender's violence. This metaphor must be presented to the offender at the time when it can have the greatest psychological impact. The therapist needs to wait for a session where there is a highly charged emotional interaction with a significant other to do the reframing of the meaning of violence in the offender's life. The criminal must make the connection between his own violence and the violence of someone he hates at a highly emotional moment, so that the reframing will be associated with someone important to him and stay in his memory. Needless to say, the therapist has to formulate this reframing many times during the therapy, but the first time has to make an impact.

Step 14: Preventing Suicide

Sex offenders are at a high risk for suicide, and the possibility of a suicide attempt cannot be underestimated. The therapist needs to give hope and show optimism that the offender can change, the child can heal, and everyone can move on to a better life. It is very important for the therapist to show respect and to show that he cares for the offender, because in some cases the offender has lost all other relationships as the result of the crime. Suicide prevention strategies should be put into effect, such as contracts with the therapist, supervision of the offender by relatives, daily contacts with the therapist, and so on.

Step 15: Finding Meaning in Life

Healing the child and doing reparation need to become the goals for the offender to give meaning to his life and to prevent suicide. He needs to understand that no one but he can do the healing, that the reparation is necessary, and that he has the power to determine what he wants the rest of his life to be. When someone has done something horrible, when the shame and the pain are unbearable, there has to be a goal that transcends the person and that gives meaning to life. Otherwise it is impossible to continue living.

Step 16: Developing Empathy and Compassion

The therapist needs to bring the biological or spiritual mother of the offender to participate in the therapy—that is, the person who has given selflessly to the offender and guided him when he was most helpless. This person can be the mother, the father, or any other person who had this significance in the offender's life. In the sessions, this "mother" will talk about her own suffering and difficulties so that feelings of empathy and compassion will arise in the offender, which can then be transferred to other people in the offender's life. When the offender is capable of feeling empathy toward one person, the therapist can guide him to transfer those feelings to others whom the offender loves. This new compassion can gradually include many people, particularly children, because they need love and protection as desperately as the offender needed it when he was a child. In this way, the therapist can work to prevent further violence.

Another strategy, developed by Jim Keim, is to have several sessions where the offender is asked to explain how other family members feel. For example, he can express how he thinks his wife feels about the abuse or other problems, then she can validate whether or not that is how she actually feels. The same can be done with every family member until everyone understands and feels for the others' situation.

It's best not to include young children in this exercise. They can observe the adults' efforts in understanding one another, but they shouldn't be put in the position where they try to understand how adults feel or to validate the adults' understanding of their own feelings.

Step 17: Fighting Loneliness

Fathers who are sex offenders are particularly ostracized by society. The therapist needs to intervene to reorganize the social network of the offender, involving relatives who are good influences, separating those who are not, and giving hope to the offender that he will some day reconnect and the loneliness will end.

Step 18: Restoration of Love

Before terminating the therapy, we must make an effort to restore some love in the offender's life, be it from his wife, his mother, or his siblings. In order to restore the mother's love it may be necessary to take her back to when the offender was a child and help her remember how much she loved him and all the sacrifices she made. We must emphasize that her job is not done and she still needs to guide and help him out. If the wife has left him, he has to be given hope that he will one day win the love of another woman.

There are usually two types of wives in this situation: the ones who turn against the offender (mentioned earlier) and the ones who turn against the victim. When the wife turns against the victim, she will sometimes prefer to expel the child from the family rather than lose the father. In these cases, our job must be to restore the mother's love for the child and keep the child in the family. The therapist can regress the mother to the time of the child's infancy and even to her pregnancy, hoping to find some core of the love she once must have had for this child. Also, the mother can be projected into the future to a time when the child will be an adult, imagining all the love and help that she can expect from this child. Sometimes the mother's rejection of the child is based on economic necessity: the fear of losing the father as breadwinner. So every effort must be made to ensure the father's financial support regardless of where he is living.

Step 19: Restoring the Offender as Protector

Before the therapy ends, the therapist needs to restore the father to a protective role in the family, the role he should always have had.

The therapist can emphasize to the family how the father will always provide financial support to the children. He can be encouraged in the sessions to speak to the children and advise them on how to avoid drugs, how to tell good friends from bad friends, and so on. The father will never again be the exclusive or primary guardian of the children, but he has to develop some kind of a protective relationship with them.

Step 20: Learning to Forgive Oneself

Many offenders suffer from intrusive thoughts and images of the abuse, haunted by the memory of what they have done and the fear of doing it again. The thoughts of what they did never leaves them, and they cannot forgive themselves.

The therapist needs to say that it's important to remember the past so we don't repeat it. The offender should never forget what he did, yet the memory shouldn't intrude at times when he needs to be occupied with other thoughts. So we ask the father how often he thinks it's necessary for him to remember what he did. The therapist then accepts the father's answer, whether it is once a day, every two days, or once a week. Then the therapist says that whenever the man remembers the abuse at more than that frequency, he immediately has to do a good deed, preferably an anonymous good deed so he doesn't get any credit for it. So the therapist helps the father identify ways in which he can do good deeds, perhaps making a donation to Children's Hospital, doing something for the elderly in the community, feeding a homeless person. The idea is that either the offender will have fewer intrusive thoughts, or he will do so many good deeds that he will begin to feel better about himself.

Basic Principles and Special Circumstances

One basic principle of our therapy is that there should be no more secrets in the family and that any notion that the victim is responsible for provoking the offender is unacceptable.

Another is that the therapist needs to carry out as many of the steps as possible given the specific circumstances of each family. But there are certain steps that absolutely must not be skipped. They are the acknowledgment of the spiritual pain, the apology on the knees, and the reparation. Even if the offender is in jail, these steps can be carried out by taking the family to visit him there. If the judge will not allow an apology session with the victim, the therapist can have the offender on his knees apologizing to the child's mother or to his parents and the grandparents on the other side. The same holds for reparation, which can always be arranged for the benefit of the victim later on in life, once no-contact orders have expired.

The same steps can be carried out in cases where the offense happened far in the past but has been discovered when the victim is already an adult. Some adults consult a therapist and tell for the first time about how they were abused as children. The therapist needs to gather as many of the relatives as possible and go through all the steps that are appropriate. If the offender is dead, someone else should not role-play his part. The issue of sexual abuse is too serious and heartbreaking for role-playing. But the other relatives can apologize to the victim for not having protected her from the abuse, even if the abuse happened twenty years ago.

If the offender has attacked a child outside the family, the same steps must be followed, with the exception that usually it's impossible to obtain permission from the court for an apology session with the victim. If this is the case, the offender can apologize to his own family for what he did and can write a letter of apology to the child that will be saved by the therapist and perhaps mailed by the offender when the victim is an adult. Also, reparation can be done in a symbolic way to an institution that represents the victim, such as a school or clinic. If the therapist is working with a victim and her family and the offender was someone outside the family, it's usually impossible to obtain the apology from the offender. But the victim's family can apologize to the victim for not having protected her from the abuser.

Group therapy with offenders is useful in helping to develop social skills and empathy, but it should not replace this crucial therapy with the family. These steps need to be carried out in relation to the family and to the victim, not in relation to strangers. The same steps can be used when there was severe physical abuse, even if there was no sexual crime, and when the offender is an uncle, grandfather, or other relative.

6

The Juvenile Sex Offender

Cloé Madanes with Dinah Smelser and James P. Keim

We have treated a large sample of adolescent male sex offenders at the Family Therapy Institute as part of a special contract with Montgomery County, Maryland. I developed the method of therapy described in the previous chapter in relation to juveniles, and then adapted it to situations where the offender is an adult. Our goal for the special project with adolescent offenders was to prevent reoffense without recourse to institutionalization.

During the first four years of the contract, from 1986 to 1990, when a case was adjudicated in court, the offender was first referred to an independent diagnostic team who decided whether the juvenile should be institutionalized or treated in outpatient therapy. If the decision was for outpatient therapy, the family was referred to us. Aside from the fact that the diagnostic team did not favor institutionalization for ideological reasons, they soon found that either the costs were prohibitive, or it was extremely difficult to find an institution that would take a juvenile sex offender. Those that specialized in sex offenders didn't want to accept them if they presented

We are grateful to Herb Goldstein, Ph.D., of the Department of Juvenile Services, State of Maryland, for conducting the outcome study on the sex offenders who were still juveniles and to Raed Mohsen, Ph.D., and Angie Steingreb, Ph.D. candidate, for following the offenders who had become adults. We wish to thank Joseph Poirier, Ph.D., of the Court Diagnostic Unit of Montgomery County, Maryland, for his collaboration and advice.

other problems, such as other forms of delinquency, drug abuse, or physical illness, and many of these boys did present such problems. The institutions that specialized in children and adolescents didn't want to accept sex offenders because they present a threat to other children. So from the beginning of the project, we were treating offenders who had been referred for institutionalization but could not be placed. Soon the county had no money at all for institutionalization and eventually no money even for the diagnostic team, which was dissolved.

The Population

Of the first eighty-one juvenile sex offenders who entered therapy between January 1987 and November 1992, six had been referred to institutionalization but could not be placed because of lack of funding. Thirty-eight of these boys were considered by the diagnostic team to be "undersocialized child exploiters" or "sexually aggressive," which are severe categories according to O'Brien's Juvenile Sex Offender Classification Scale (1985).

All eighty-one sex offenders were males, ranging from age seven to twenty. (There was one seven-year-old and one twenty-year-old.) Forty-four percent were between the ages of twelve and fifteen, and 44 percent were between the ages of sixteen and eighteen. The racial composition was 47 percent white, 30 percent black, 20 percent Hispanic, and 3 percent Asian American.

Most of the offenders (90 percent) were living in the home of at least one biological parent at the time of the offense. Fifty-seven percent were living with two parents (including one stepparent).

Almost 50 percent of the offenders were considered learning disabled, 26 percent suffered from serious health problems, and 13 percent had language disorders. Twenty-five percent had histories of disruptive behavior at school or truancy.

Contrary to what could have been expected, only 12 percent had been seriously neglected in early childhood. Less than 20 percent had no contact with their biological fathers. Almost 20 percent had been in therapy previous to the sexual offense and before the referral to our institute.

Substance abuse was considered to be a problem for 33 percent of the juvenile offenders. Twenty-three percent had committed other delinquent acts previous to the sexual offenses.

Almost 40 percent of the juveniles related that they had been sexually abused previous to committing their offenses, but we suspect that many more had had some kind of premature sexual initiation. Most often (53 percent of the time) the abuser was an unrelated male. Older brothers perpetrated the abuse in 19 percent of the cases, fathers in 19 percent, and stepfathers in 8 percent of the cases.

Physical abuse of the juvenile offender was reported or known to have occurred in 20 percent of the sample. The abuser was most often the biological father (57 percent). Mothers were perpetrators of the abuse in 14 percent of the cases, and stepmothers in 14 percent of the cases.

Sixteen percent of the offenders had made suicide threats or attempts. In more than 30 percent of the families it was known that there were other cases of sexual abuse. There had been violence between various family members in 39 percent of the offenders' families. Violence between parental figures was reported in 23 percent of the cases. Substance abuse was a problem in 33 percent of the families.

Forty-five percent of the families lived in poverty, had been impoverished during most of the offender's life, or were suffering from unemployment. Thirty-three percent of the families reported that they were very religious.

To summarize, relatively high proportions of the eighty-one juvenile sex offenders had been subjected to sexual and/or physical abuse or to other family violence and/or exhibited behavioral problems (school problems, substance abuse, and previous criminal offenses). A large percentage were impoverished, were learning disabled, and suffered from health problems.

The Crimes

Sixty percent of the offenders were referred for offenses against one victim, 21 percent for offenses against two victims, and 19 percent for offenses against three or more victims. The most common behaviors were fondling (43 percent) and vaginal penetration (30 percent). Oral stimulation occurred in 23 percent of the cases and anal penetration in 20 percent. Offenders with three or more victims tended to choose victims of both sexes at a greater rate than did less chronic offenders.

Nearly all of the victims were younger than twelve years old at the time of the offense. The largest groups of victims by age were three- to five-year-olds (21 percent), five- to seven-year-olds (21 percent), and ten- to twelve-year-olds (20 percent), with the total age range of victims spanning from younger than three to seventeen (only 3 percent of the victims were adults).

Most often (in 40 percent of the cases), the victim was a nonrelated child known to the offender. The second most common victim-offender relationship was with blood-related children (33 percent); most often these victims were younger full or half-siblings, and occasionally they were cousins.

The Therapy

The method of therapy consisted of the same steps described for adult offenders in the previous chapter. The first seven steps are the same. The therapist gathers the family for a first session and talks to each one about what they know about the sexual crime. Then the therapist asks the offender why what he did was wrong and discusses the spiritual pain that he inflicted on the victim and on the family. The offender expresses his sorrow and repentance on his knees to the victim.

Step 8 differs in that, instead of asking only the mother to apologize on her knees to the victim for not having protected her, the therapist asks both parents and the siblings to apologize on their knees to the victim for not having protected her or him from the offender. This is usually done by asking the whole family to kneel in front of the victim and for each to say a few words about their sorrow for not having prevented the abuse. Whenever possible, the therapist brings in the grandparents to also apologize, even if only because they could have had better communication with the victim, so that the victim would have told them what she was going through.

In step 9, the parents discuss what the future consequences would be should the offender commit another sexual crime, and the therapist encourages them to settle for the harshest consequences. The offender will be expelled from the family, placed in an institution or with relatives. Another crime, or even the suspicion of any sexual wrongdoing, cannot happen again. When there is a single parent, other relatives may be involved or the single parent may decide alone on future consequences.

In step 10, a protector for the victim is identified and engaged in similar ways as to when the offender is the father. Step 11, reparation, also has to take place. The parents decide on something that the juvenile will do that will take considerable sacrifice and a considerable period of time, to do reparation to the victim. The juvenile might work and deposit a certain amount of money every month in an account in the name of the victim, toward her future education; or he might give up a precious possession and donate it to charity.

In step 12, the discussion of sexuality, it's best to have a session with the father (or a father figure) and the juvenile, and to ask this man to explain male sexuality to the boy. The father usually has sexual problems himself and, in having to talk to his son, is often able to come to terms with his own problems. The therapist encourages repression and asks the offender to follow certain steps when the wrong sexual impulse strikes, in the same way as for adult offenders.

With juveniles, there is one special difficulty, however, and that is that a therapist cannot legally encourage any kind of sexual activity with others because sex with a minor can be construed to be statutory rape. Recommending masturbation is often also a problem since many of these families are Christian Fundamentalists who oppose masturbation. So the therapist often ends by recommending that the adolescent take long showers and wash carefully in certain places, hoping that he will take the hint as to what he can do when he has some privacy in the shower.

With the victim, the therapist encourages the perspective that the victimization, although horrible and traumatic, will not be the major event in her life, that it has not transformed her into a different kind of person—a victim. The therapist makes every effort to put the abuse in the perspective of all the other things that happen in a person's life that are much more important. The emphasis is on how the child did nothing to provoke it and is not to blame. It's like being hit by a truck when you're walking on the sidewalk.

With juveniles, in step 13, the metaphor to discover is sometimes only about sexual abuse and not about physical violence, since some of the juvenile offenders are not physically violent. The therapist needs to explain that sexual abuse is violence even when it doesn't involve physical injury.

Step 14, the restoration of the mother's love (or the father's) is important. Some parents reject the offender and some the victim. It's particularly painful for the therapist to work with situations where the parents reject the victim. In both cases, the therapist must make every effort to restore the parents' love. When the parents reject the victim, the therapist must emphasize how she was not to blame and explain the seduction and coercion involved in sexual abuse. The parents must understand how they developed a distance from the child, not through any fault of the child but precisely because the child was abused and afraid. The therapist needs to take them back to a time when they remember how much they loved this child.

When the parents reject the offender, the therapist makes every effort to bring out his good qualities, emphasizing that the abuse is just one aspect of his behavior, that it will not persist, and that he has other good qualities. The parents also need to go back in time to when the offender was lovable so they can build on that love they once had for the child.

Before ending the therapy, the offender's position in the family must be restored so that he can again be in the position of an older brother. He will never be trusted again with the children, but the therapist can have him advise the younger children about how to avoid violence and drugs, how to tell if friends are good, and so on. The juvenile offender must also be encouraged to forgive himself and to develop empathy and compassion.

When the victim is outside the family, it's best to do everything possible to obtain the court's permission to have an apology session with the victim and her family. The offender should apologize on his knees, not just to the victim but to her parents (and/or other relatives) as well. This is particularly important with juveniles because usually the victim is a neighbor, a child that goes to the same school as the offender, or a member of the same church community, so chances are that the offender and the victim will continue to see each other. For this reason, a public apology is necessary to prevent the victim from being fearful and ashamed in the presence of the offender.

When an apology in person is not possible, it should be done in the form of a letter. Reparation also needs to take place, directly to the victim or symbolically by donating money, time, or effort to a charitable organization.

The essential aspects of the method are to make sure that the juvenile takes full responsibility for his crime, that he understands the spiritual pain that he inflicted, that he is truly repentant, that he apologizes in public, and that he does reparation.

Apart from family and individual sessions, all juveniles participated in group therapy, which is particularly helpful in various ways.

The group puts pressure on each offender to take responsibility for his crime, discouraging secrecy and denial. A great deal of the focus of the group therapy is on developing social skills, which are very necessary since these young men are usually undersocialized and disagreeable toward adults as well as toward their peers. That is, the group focuses on helping the youths behave so that they will be liked and appreciated instead of being rejected and feared. Developing empathy and compassion is also an important focus of the group therapy.

In the group, the boys discuss sexuality. They look at popular movies about abuse, violence, and social problems, which become the focus of discussion. Nonviolence as a source of power is an important theme. The therapists sometimes take the group to stores, parks, and other public places to focus on appropriate social behavior. There is a great deal of discussion about their relationship with their mothers, their concerns, and their frustration about not being able to help their mothers as much as they want to.

The Outcome

For seventy-two of seventy-five cases that were closed by November 1, 1992, we were able to obtain follow-up information for a period of at least two years after termination of therapy. Among this group, there were only three repeat offenses. This is a success rate of 96 percent, in the sense of no repeat offense.

Fifty-nine of the juveniles had been referred originally by the Department of Juvenile Services, and this department followed up on them for a minimum of two years after the termination of therapy; of these juveniles, there were only two repeat offenders. The remaining thirteen juveniles were followed through contacts with the Department of Social Services and through independent contacts with the offenders' families made by research assistants. Sixty-two offenders were already adults by the end of 1994. They were followed through independent examination of adult court records. Only one had reoffended, and the charge was indecent exposure.

Twenty-three of the juveniles entered therapy in 1987–1988, and thirty-three started therapy in 1989–1990. So a total of fifty-six of the juveniles were followed by therapists for at least five years.

In 39 percent of the cases the duration of therapy was one year or less. The sessions were once a week for the first few months, gradually becoming every other week, and eventually once a month. Every effort was made to continue some therapeutic contact for as long as possible to prevent any possibility of reoffense.

The data on recidivism were based not only on court conviction records but also on offenders' self-reports, reports from parents or parole counselors, children's protective services reports, and actual arrests. Treatment data on each youth were obtained by reviewing treatment files and by direct communication with the therapists.

Twenty-three juveniles reoffended in some criminal manner other than sexual abuse. Of these, sixty-five percent of the crimes involved theft, breaking and entering, or trespass. The other reoffenders were charged with assault or illegal possession of weapons. There was only one case of drug-related charges. There were no suicide attempts after therapy started. Only one of the twenty-three victims who were blood-related child siblings has not been reintegrated into the nuclear family. None of these children who were victims have become sexual offenders themselves.

These results are particularly interesting in light of the fact that more than 50 percent of the offenders suffered from poverty, family violence, substance abuse by themselves or other family members, learning disabilities, and serious health problems. Also, the results are interesting considering that during the initial assessment, 73 percent of the offenders refused to take responsibility for their offenses, and 83 percent showed no signs of remorse for their crimes.

* * * * * * *

The following are some case examples of therapies conducted by Dinah Smelser, LCSW, who was responsible for the therapy of forty young men. These cases required a special effort and special consideration on the part of the therapist. The steps were all carried out in all of the cases, but what will be emphasized here in these examples are the exceptions to the steps and the special circumstances of each case.

The Congregation

Paul, a pastor, and his wife, Mary, had been foster parents for many years. Despite their wishes to have their own children, Mary could not become pregnant, so eventually they adopted Bill when he was three years old. He had been removed from his mother, who was a drug addict and a prostitute, at eighteen months of age. He had lived with a foster mother to whom he became very attached and whom he could still remember when he was sixteen years old. When he was about three and a half years old, he was adopted by the pastor and his wife. At that time, parental rights with his biological mother were finally terminated. Two years later, a little girl was born to Paul and Mary.

When Bill was fourteen years old, a cousin in Mary's family, a four-year-old boy, revealed to his mother that he had been sexually abused by Bill for about a year. The abuse had occurred during family vacations when the four-year-old would visit Paul and Mary and stay with them for periods of one or two weeks. The abuse consisted of oral and anal sexual acts performed by Bill on the little boy.

Paul and Mary were shocked. They had never suspected that Bill could be capable of such acts. They consulted a private counselor, and Bill was in individual therapy for one year, but there was no family therapy. During this time, Paul was concerned because Bill continued to be upset and appeared withdrawn and isolated. Finally one evening, he went into his son's room and said, "I know that you have done this to another child."

He really didn't know that, but he felt that more had to be disclosed. Bill then revealed that he had also molested his parents' best friends' child, another four-year-old boy with whom the family would frequently visit. This family was part of the congregation that Paul and Mary ministered to. Bill said that he had stopped this abuse when the other abuse was discovered.

With this revelation, Paul realized that he had to call the police again. After the first case of abuse, the court had allowed him to seek private counseling for Bill, so the abuse had been kept secret within the family. Now the parents of this child had to be notified. They insisted that the abuse should be revealed to the whole congregation, which they immediately proceeded to do.

When Bill and his family were referred to our program by the court, our therapist Dinah had to deal not only with the abuse of the two young children but also with the fact that the congregation was up in arms because the first abuse had not been revealed to them a year earlier.

Bill is a gifted musician who was the organist and pianist of the church. He had been working in Sunday school, and the congregation felt that he could have abused other children. They were furious at the pastor and his wife for not alerting them after the first abuse was discovered. Paul and Mary had not revealed the first abuse because they believed they had Bill under strict supervision, and they didn't think he would molest another child.

So in this case, the therapist had to plan apologies not only to the two victims and their families but also to the whole congregation. Three months after the initiation of therapy with Dinah, a congregational meeting had been called. It was a process nomination because the parishioners believed that there should be an open forum for people's concerns. The pastor would probably lose his position as pastor if this meeting were not handled correctly.

By the time this meeting was called, Bill and his parents had already apologized to the cousin's family for the first abuse. Bill was extremely remorseful, which is very common with sex offenders, particularly juveniles, as soon as they understand the spiritual pain they caused in their victims. He said he had not disclosed the second abuse for fear that his parents would break down. Mary had, in fact, almost collapsed physically and emotionally when the first abuse was discovered, and as a consequence of this initial abuse, she had been ostracized by her family.

This breakup between Mary and her family had been going on for a year by the time the family therapy with Dinah began. So Bill felt that his mother would go absolutely crazy if she learned of another abuse. He said that was why he had kept the secret, even though he had stopped the abuse of the second child when the first abuse was discovered. The second child's family did not believe this, however, and thought that the abuse had continued until Bill had confessed to his father. Bill was very remorseful and apologized very sincerely to his parents and to his little sister for the pain he had caused them.

When the therapy was beginning to focus on the step of reparation, the father told Dinah about the meeting of the congregation that was being planned to expel him. He had asked for leave of absence for six weeks because there was so much anger directed at him that he felt he couldn't do his ministerial work. Another minister had come in to take on his duties.

In discussing the congregational meeting in therapy, the parents said that they would be present to answer to the congregation. Bill insisted that he wanted to be present also and to publicly apologize to everyone for the pain he had caused them.

The congregational meeting went on for three hours, during which everyone who had concerns was allowed to speak. Bill and his parents listened. The second victim's father was there, and at the end of the meeting he stood up and directly accused Bill of not being remorseful, of not being sorry for what he had done. Dinah had not been able to arrange an apology session with this victim's family because of orders for no contact from the court. So the victim's father had never heard what Bill had to say.

Dinah had prepared Bill, helping him express what he wanted to say. He had carefully written it down. This was a very emotional situation for him, and he wanted to be careful about how he expressed himself.

He stood up in front of 100 people and poured out his heart directly to the victim's father, expressing his sorrow for all the pain he had caused the child and the family, and his sorrow to the congregation who had always been loving and accepting of him. Bill's words were deeply moving to most of the people present, yet it was decided that the congregation would have a vote of confidence in the minister and whether they wanted him to continue. It took a year for that vote of confidence to take place, for the healing to occur in that congregation, even though Paul had been a minister in that church for fifteen years. Until the father was accepted back as minister to the congregation, Bill did not return to the church.

After two years of therapy, Dinah obtained permission from the court to have an apology session with the second child who was molested and his family. They were only ready to listen to Bill after he had written several letters to the parents and to the child expressing his remorse. Both victims' parents did not want Bill to do reparation to their children, so he decided to work on Saturdays for a computer company and to donate the money from this job to sponsor a child through the Save the Children Foundation.

Nothing Happened

A special problem in therapy is when the offender and the family deny that any abuse has happened, even after the case has been adjudicated by court. This was the problem that Dinah faced with Louis and his mother.

When a referral came to us from our county, the case had been already adjudicated by the court and the juvenile had pleaded "involved." Juveniles don't plead guilty—they plead "involved," and there is some declaration by the court as to whether the charge is true or not.

Louis was fifteen years old when he allegedly sexually molested five young boys in his apartment complex over a period of six months, with eye witnesses attesting to this fact, including the victims, who were five to eight years old. The children did not appear in court because Louis pleaded involved at the time of the court hearing. That is, he said he did commit the sexual acts.

However, by the first time he came to therapy with his single mother, Ella, and his grandmother, he was denying that he had ever done anything. So in the first step, when Dinah asked for an account of the sex offense, Louis said that nothing had happened, Ella said that nothing had happened, and the grandmother said that nothing had happened. But Dinah had a very thick police report relating all the things that had actually happened.

Louis's older brother was already in jail serving a long sentence for sexual assault and drug abuse. Ella and the grandmother told Dinah what a wonderful boy Louis was, and Dinah could sense that they had put all their hope in this second child. He would be the first person in the family to graduate from high school. Louis was the son who would pull the family out of poverty. Dinah could feel the tremendous pressure that Louis felt to not let his mother down. Louis and Ella had a very close relationship, probably exacerbated by the fact that Louis had a learning disability and was somewhat slow, of borderline intelligence.

So when Dinah faced what actually happened, as detailed in the police report, and the subsequent denial by the family, she began to pick out certain events from the police report and present them to the family. She pointed out that a certain child had said that a sexual act took place and a witness had also said it actually had happened. But upon each disclosure from the report, Louis would say, "No, I didn't do it; it didn't happen." Ella said he had been raised well and trained well and had even cared responsibly for younger cousins in the past. She just couldn't believe any of this was true.

After feeling stymied for some time, Dinah came to see me. Following my suggestion, she said to the family that since Louis had led people to be suspicious of him and caused all these allegations to come upon him, he needed to apologize for leading people to have these thoughts about his behavior. So in this way, Dinah could begin to do the work of going through the steps. She addressed the humiliation and the shame that Louis had caused in his mother and grandmother for having all these people believe these things about him.

A special problem was that the court had ordered that Louis could have no contact with any child under twelve years of age. Since the mother didn't believe this was important because nothing had happened, she wasn't particularly careful, and there were children going in and out of the home, young cousins whom Louis was still having contact with. So Dinah said to the mother and grandmother that because Louis had behaved in ways that led to all the accusations, it was important for him not to be falsely accused again. The women needed to help him by supervising him closely so he would never be left alone with a child under twelve and so he wouldn't have the opportunity to behave again in ways that could lead to further accusations. Mother and grandmother agreed that this was important since they didn't want Louis to be accused again. Dinah was able to arrange then for supervision twenty-four hours a day. Louis couldn't go outside of the house without being accompanied by an older adult, so he couldn't hang out around the apartment complex or go to the pool unsupervised. Louis agreed that it was important for people not to tell bad stories about him, so he accepted the supervision.

Dinah had the mother explain to Louis what behaviors would lead to accusations and what were good behaviors that would cause people to say good things about him. The discussion was very specific and concrete about what were the things he should not be doing and what were the things he should be doing so his reputation could be restored. Every day his mother and grandmother were to ask him how he had behaved in school and if he had treated people nicely or if he had touched anyone in any inappropriate way. The women told him that he should not touch anyone at all, even in jest, that he should keep his hands to himself.

The therapy proceeded like this for several months with Louis still saying that nothing had happened, but with mother and grandmother supervising him strictly. Then Dinah decided to include

Louis in the group therapy for juvenile sex offenders that was regularly conducted at the institute as part of the juvenile sex offender program. When a new member joins the group, the routine is for each boy to disclose to the new person what offense they committed to be part of the group. Then the new youth has to do the same and disclose his offense. When it was his turn, Louis said that he was in the group because he had been accused, even though he had not done anything wrong. The other boys didn't like to hear this.

"We don't believe you, Louis. We don't believe you didn't do anything. Come on, tell us what you did!"

Louis continued to deny at first, but after a few sessions in the group, he admitted that the accusations were true.

After the group session where Louis admitted to what he had done, Dinah asked him if now he would be able to tell the truth to his mother and grandmother. He said that he would, and in the next family session, he did. He said to his mother that he just couldn't say the truth and let her down, and that's why he had denied and kept the secret all this time. The mother forgave him and said that his behavior had been so exemplary in the last year that she trusted him that he would never molest anyone again.

The therapy proceeded with acts of reparation and apology letters to all the victims. His mother helped him to write the letters in the sessions, even though none could be delivered because of no-contact orders.

The Abused Abuser

Don was seventeen years old when he first came to therapy. He had been abandoned by his mother in the Philippines at age four or five due to extreme poverty. The mother vanished, never to be found again. He never knew his father. Don went to live with a maternal aunt from ages five to eight until she no longer could support him, also due to extreme poverty. At age eight he was legally adopted by his maternal grandparents, who had relocated in Oregon. The grandmother was warm to Don, but the grandfather was very strict, harsh, and distant.

Don remembered that from ages eleven to fifteen he was sexually abused by his grandfather's brother, who would come to the house to spend weekends on a regular basis. He would go into Don's room at night, often sleeping in Don's bed and molesting him. Don could not understand why the grandparents never did anything about this behavior. The uncle had told him never to tell anyone, so he didn't, but he was confused and felt that there was something wrong with him that this was happening to him.

A great part of his confusion had to do with the fact that many times his grandmother would see his great-uncle coming out of Don's room in the morning but wouldn't say anything. He was so afraid of his grandfather that he never said anything to him or to his grandmother. Clearly there had been a collusion between the grandparents and the great-uncle and a very strong mandate of secrecy. No one talked about the sexual molestation. In addition, Don's grandfather was physically abusive of him and extremely demanding, making him do all kinds of work.

At age fifteen, Don was able to arrange to come to live with an aunt's family in Maryland (the youngest sister of the biological mother). She was a very loving, kind person who had two little boys ages one and three. After one month at the aunt's house, Don started to sexually abuse the older boy. When they came to therapy, the oldest was five and the youngest was three. They were extremely bright and articulate and were able to describe the abuse very clearly to Dinah.

The parents of the boys had begun to suspect something by the time their oldest son, Johnny, was four, when he had already been abused for a period of one year. He had started saying things to the father like, "Don kisses my teetee," and he would try to touch his father in sexual ways. Johnny would also masturbate all the time.

Don had been left in charge of the children every afternoon while the mother and father worked. Mother would leave around three in the afternoon, and Father would come home at six, so when Don came home from high school, he would be in charge of the children until the father came home, and this was his opportunity to abuse the children. He never abused the younger child, but everything he did to Johnny was in the presence of the youngest child.

When the father confronted Don, he said no, he had never done such a thing. He was so believable in his denial that they continued to allow him to watch the children, even though Johnny had tried in many ways to disclose to the father what had happened.

The father had been sexually abused himself as a child, and he just couldn't face the possibility that this could be happening to his children. Another month went by with Johnny continuing to say things, and finally the father confronted the nephew, who said yes, he did commit the abuse.

Upon this disclosure, the family came to therapy. Don was suicidal after the disclosure, so they were sent to therapy by the county even before the evaluation was completed. Don was extremely afraid that he would be rejected and abandoned. He didn't want to go back to his grandparents', and he was afraid that he would just be expelled from the home. Because he was by this time seventeen, he was charged as an adult, plead guilty to a fourth degree sex offense, and was found guilty, ordered to therapy, and put on probation for five years.

From the beginning of the therapy Don was extremely remorseful but not so much because he felt the pain of the young children. He felt his own pain. At first there was a great deal of minimization on his part. He said, for example, that he committed the abuse only two or three times. But the more that was said, the more he admitted, until he finally admitted that it had been going on for more than one year. At first he said he had just touched the child, but later he admitted to committing oral sex on the little boy and to having the child perform oral sex on him and masturbate him. This would usually take place in the boys' bedroom with the younger child watching from the crib.

By the time they came to therapy, the parents were extremely angry. However, after listening to Don's expressions of sorrow and repentance and to his apologies, they agreed to let him stay in their home until he finished high school (he was already a senior). Then he would have to find another place to live.

Don had been working during high school and by the time he graduated he was an assistant manager of a fast-food restaurant. So with the aunt and uncle's help, he was able to find an apartment that he shared with two older co-workers.

The father of the little boys told Don in the second session that he himself had been raped at age twelve by an older man, and he had always wanted to protect his children. He couldn't believe that he had trusted Don, and Don had betrayed him, abusing his children when they had been so generous as to offer him a home. Don had not revealed his own abuse. But in this second session, after the boys' father talked about being raped, the aunt said she had also been sexually abused by the same great-uncle who had molested Don. Then Don disclosed that this man had abused him sexually for four years. He also told that from ages four to six, when he was living with another aunt, he was sadistically molested by her. If he wet the bed, she would force him to collect his urine and drink it. This probably was one of many experiences of humiliation and shame that he was put through as a child.

By the time the case went to court, there was a no-contact order between Don and the two boys, except for the therapy sessions. Don was living in an apartment. The uncle continued to be angry with him, but the aunt forgave him and so did Johnny.

During the therapy, Don decided that his goal would be to prevent other children from being abused. So he wanted to confront the great-uncle who had abused him because he was convinced he was abusing other children in the family, perhaps even his own. Dinah contacted the authorities in Oregon who said that Don would have to visit that state to report it, but Don didn't have the money. So he called his grandparents and revealed the abuse to them over the phone. There was another child in the family who was now an adult but still lived in Oregon with the grandparents. Don talked with her over the phone, and she said that she had been sexually abused by the same great-uncle but had never revealed it to anyone. As a result of this conversation, however, she told the grandparents and reported the uncle.

They decided to have a family meeting to which the great-uncle was invited, and not only was he confronted with what he had done to her, but they also presented a letter from Don with a description of what he had done to him. The great-uncle denied having done anything ever. But the grandparents believed Don, even though he had always thought that they somehow knew but would never admit that it was true. The fact that the grandfather confronted his brother, taking Don's side, went a long way toward healing Don and repairing his relationship with his grandfather. It was the beginning of a renewed relationship between Don and both grandparents.

Six months later, the grandmother died of a heart attack. Don and his aunt went to the funeral, and, at that time, he talked to his grandfather about the abuse, and the grandfather apologized to him for not having protected him. Don continued to address each situation of abuse in his life, including the physical abuse by the grandfather. With every revelation, his self-esteem improved and he became stronger. As he was able to address his own victimization, he was able to develop compassion for the children that he himself had abused. The uncle in Oregon was never prosecuted but the family had been warned, so he couldn't easily abuse other children in the family.

Johnny's father didn't want Don to do any reparation to his child. So the family agreed that as reparation, Johnny would send $50 every five weeks to an aunt who was a single mother raising five children in poverty in the Philippines. In this way, he would be helping other children to escape some of what he had endured. Don took on this responsibility willingly and also wrote frequently to the aunt to keep in touch as to how the children were doing.

Johnny's father never forgave Don and didn't want to see him outside of the therapy sessions, but he accepted that his wife felt differently and that she kept an ongoing relationship with Don.

When the probationary period was over, Don went back to Oregon to live with his grandfather. At that point he had made some friends and even had a girlfriend, but he wanted to be with his grandfather. After a year, however, he had lost his job and decided to come back to Maryland. He came to see Dinah to tell her he was doing fine and he visited with his aunt.

Johnny never behaved inappropriately with other children at school, in the community, or with the younger brother. The parents collaborated in the therapy, had long conversations with Johnny, and supervised him carefully until they were convinced that he would be alright.

A great part of the therapy consisted in focusing on Don's strengths: all that he had survived and how resourceful and hard-working he was. When he was overcome by the realization of how he had harmed the little boys, Dinah encouraged him to look up in the library the lives of people who had suffered a great deal in their childhood and youth and yet had grown to be successful. He was also encouraged to write his own story of survival as an inspiration to others in the future.

The Secret

Raymond was age twelve when he raped a female schoolmate on school grounds. His father was a business executive, his mother a housewife. The parents had been married for seventeen years. Each parent had children from a previous marriage, but Raymond was the only child from this union. The other children were all very successful: two were married, one was in the service. They described the family as very close. All the older children doted on Raymond. He was the child that his older brother and sisters loved the most.

The family was confused by the allegations against Raymond.

He was an achieving student in advanced classes. He was on the football team, always respectful to his parents, and very close to his father, for whom he was the only male child. When the parents heard the charges, they just couldn't believe that their child had done this. The father had had open conversations with Raymond about sex and had told him he would always be willing to answer any questions. He had instructed him about AIDS and condoms and felt they had a relationship where they could talk about anything.

The female schoolmate that he raped, Sandra, was fourteen years old. Raymond said in the first session that he and Sandra had jokingly talked about having intercourse, and he was confused because he thought that she was in agreement with this. The police report didn't state that at all. One of the reasons Raymond thought it was consensual was that the previous year they had had oral sex in a school bathroom and had been found by another student. The parents were never told about this, even though the guidance counselor had talked to both children. The parents were incensed. Had they known a year prior that this was going on, they said, they would have been able to do something about it. Now their son had been charged with rape.

The only clue that the parents had of anything unusual was that Raymond's grades had begun to fall and he had started to act out in class, becoming the clown, the center of attention with his antics. The parents thought that Raymond wanted to be a big shot in school. In the first session, Raymond said that one of the reasons he wanted to have sex was to say he was no longer a virgin.

The sexual act took place in the school hallway, behind a movable partition, during lunchtime. A student came by, saw the whole episode, and reported to the principal. Raymond was arrested, and Sandra was taken to the hospital where she said that he had actually grabbed her as she was walking by in the hallway, and she had told him no, many times. He had put on a condom, engaged in forcible sex standing up, and had been very angry and aggressive during the whole interchange. The condom was found later in the hallway.

During the first session, Raymond was extremely upset. The family had initiated therapy at the institute before the case actually went through the court system. The father and Raymond had not spoken since the rape had occurred. The father was very upset. He couldn't believe his son had done this. No son of his could ever do such a thing. The mother's greatest concern was the deterioration of the relationship between father and son.

Raymond was removed from the school until a decision was made about where he would be placed. So he was being tutored at home. He took responsibility for his wrongful behavior although he still acted confused about whether it was consensual or whether it was rape. He acknowledged that she said no, but he had thought she really wanted it. So he was blaming her for this encounter. Probably part of the confusion was that the previous year she had consented to the oral sexual act.

Raymond apologized to his parents, but the father said he didn't trust him and wasn't sure he could believe his apology. The father said he couldn't forgive him. So Raymond had to find a way to convince his father that he could be trusted again. He apologized to him every day for what he had done and for the lack of trust that had resulted. After a couple of weeks of daily apologies, the father began to engage with Raymond and to talk in the family therapy sessions. Until then, he had come to the sessions but wouldn't say anything.

Raymond pleaded guilty to the involvement of second degree rape. There was a no-contact order, but he wrote a letter of apology to Sandra. He was put on probation and ordered to therapy. The family decided that Raymond's reparation would consist of helping his mother, who did a great deal of volunteer work for shelters for abused women. Raymond began to help her sort clothes for the shelters.

Raymond did well in therapy. He seemed to understand why

what he had done was wrong. He took responsibility in court, telling the judge that at first he'd thought that the victim had consented but now he understood that when she said no, he should have stopped. The father and Raymond reconciled, and everything seemed to be going well.

One day the mother asked to see Dinah alone. One of the issues that had always bothered the mother was that the father had come from a very good, intact family, while the mother had several brothers who were in jail. She had escaped this family, but she was concerned that her son was doing some of the things that her brothers had been accused of. She was worried that Raymond was in some way identifying with these uncles.

When Dinah was puzzled about why the mother was so concerned, she finally said that one of the things they hadn't told Dinah was that Raymond was adopted and his biological father was her brother. They had adopted Raymond as an infant when his father, one of the brothers who was then in jail, had fathered a child with a woman who was a drug addict. Raymond's mother had been physically abusive to him. She said that when they got Raymond, there were cigarette burns on his body and he was suffering from failure to thrive. Her husband had serious doubts about wanting this child, feeling that they were older, they had teenage children, and he was worried about future repercussions. But the mother convinced him to do it. The whole family knew, including the older three children, and they all agreed to keep it a secret from Raymond. As he grew older, they realized that they should tell him, but they were afraid that he would identify with his biological father. So by the time he was eight, they relocated and cut off ties with the mother's family, for fear that Raymond would discover the adoption.

Now the parents were thinking that they should reveal the adoption to Raymond, because the biological father had come out of jail and was saying that he wanted to tell Raymond. He was having second thoughts about his decision to give him up for adoption. The greatest fear and the biggest secret in the family was that

Raymond was adopted and the father was a criminal. The father's greatest fear was that Raymond would no longer consider him his father.

The mother told Dinah that she and her husband had decided that Raymond should be told. Dinah arranged a family session where the father would speak to Raymond. The mother said she couldn't tell him, but she would be available for any questions he might have after the revelation. The brother and sisters were out of town but would be available to talk to him on the phone. Everybody had felt that it was necessary to tell him now because they knew that Raymond had suspicions. He had begun to ask for his birth certificate. He would comment about how much he looked like his mother, but not like his dad. Raymond was very short, and the father was very tall. All the uncles were very short.

When the adoption was revealed, it was clear that Raymond had never suspected that he was adopted. But he had known there was something they weren't telling him. He had felt a distance from the parents that he couldn't understand. He knew there was something he didn't know.

Raymond accepted the adoption. The parents said they felt guilty about keeping this secret from Raymond after they had asked him to reveal everything. It was a way of saying to him that there would be no more family secrets. He could also tell them everything that was going on with him.

Until then, Raymond had had a great deal of trouble communicating and negotiating with his parents. He could never ask them for anything. After the revelation, that barrier was broken. Before the secret was revealed, the parents had been very strict in limiting Raymond's social involvement with peers. Afterward, he was able to negotiate privileges and to have an easier social life. Dinah suspected that a good part of the expression of anger against Sandra had been related to the secret.

With Dinah's encouragement, Raymond reassured the parents that they were his real parents, and the parents reassured Raymond that he was their real child. A year later, everyone was well, and there had been no further incidents.

Two years later, at the age of fifteen, Raymond was charged with second-degree rape by his girlfriend, a seventeen-year-old school-mate. He had forced himself on her, and he had done it once again on school grounds, in the football field. He argued that he had mis-understood her and thought that she had consented to intercourse. Raymond was sent to a correctional institution and will resume fam-ily therapy when he comes home. He is one of the three juveniles in our sample who reoffended.

The Fractured Family

Tim was twelve years old when he was charged with the attempted rape of a six-year-old girl from his neighborhood. Tim lived with his single-parent mother, a maternal aunt, and her two teenage chil-dren in a two-bedroom apartment.

The mother had a very abusive alcoholic boyfriend who period-ically beat her and Tim. They had been a homeless threesome prior to moving in with the aunt. They would find shelter in abandoned buildings at night. Tim went to school during the day, using a false address, but he had no home for approximately a year. He suffered from a very bad case of neglect and abuse.

When he was evaluated by the county, Tim disclosed that he had molested three younger male cousins. These children were two, four, and six years old. Two years prior to that, he had abused a lit-tle female cousin at the home of his grandparents.

Tim had never met his biological father, who was in jail for the attempted rape of his own sister, who was retarded. When the grandmother revealed that Tim's father, her son, had attempted to rape his sister, Tim's father had tried to kill her. So he was in jail for both the attempted rape of his sister and the attempted murder of his own mother.

Because of Tim's history and lack of family stability, the county was recommending residential placement but wanted therapy prior to his placement. Later they decided they just didn't have enough money for residential placement, so the outpatient therapy at the institute would continue. But he was considered at high risk to re-offend unless some structure was put in place so he could remain in the community.

Tim's mother was marginal in terms of her feelings toward him. She loved Tim, but she was upfront in saying that she wasn't willing to do what was necessary to keep him connected to her. She was angry at him for the bad things he had done and, if the court wanted to place him, she wasn't going to stop them. But Dinah was able to get her cooperation in terms of coming to therapy.

The county put Tim on an electronic monitor so his whereabouts were known at all times. He couldn't leave his mother's house except for going to school and for visiting his grandparents. A male teacher at school gave him special tutoring and functioned as a special mentor and friend to Tim. The grandparents were notified of the abuse that had occurred in the past and warned to supervise Tim closely during his visits.

In the first session, Tim told his mother about all the children he had molested. His aunt, the mother of the three little abused children, was invited to the second session, and Tim apologized to her for the abuse of her children. There was a no-contact order with those children and with all children under a certain age, so Tim wrote letters of apology to all the children he had molested. At a later date, Dinah was able to collaborate with the therapist of the little boys, so it was arranged for Tim to have a session with those children and apologize to them.

The six-year-old for whose attempted rape Tim had first been charged had moved with her mother out of the community and could not be located to arrange any kind of apology. However, with the help of his mother, Tim wrote letters of apology to that mother and child, which he kept. He had one that he kept in his pocket in case he ever saw her. He was quite remorseful.

It later was revealed that while they had been homeless, Tim had been sexually abused numerous times by an older teenager and raped anally when he was nine years old. There was very little supervision by the mother at the time, and he was left many times alone roaming the streets. He revealed this very tearfully in a session and expressed the fear that this experience would reflect on his own sexuality. He feared becoming a homosexual because this had happened to him. This is a common fear in boys who have been abused by older men. He was very embarrassed to talk about this with his mother.

By the time therapy was terminated a year and a half later, the mother was taking a little more interest in Tim. He had always wanted to be close to her and had always felt rejected and unprotected. She revealed that she had been sexually attacked herself when they were homeless.

As a result of the therapy, the mother not only became closer to Tim, but she also grew closer to her parents and decided to move near them. Tim now had friends, even girlfriends, and by the end of the therapy many sessions were spent with the mother explaining to the son what type of behavior was appropriate with a girlfriend.

Tim participated enthusiastically in the group therapy. In the sessions it was made clear to the boys that their behavior had to be exemplary because they would always be under scrutiny in the community and always be at risk of being suspects when a sexual crime occurs. To date, Tim has not presented any suspicious behavior, and his involvement with girls is a good sign that he may have caught up with his normal developmental stage.

The group therapy was very helpful to Tim in being able to reveal the abuse that he himself suffered, because in the group he heard the other boys talk about what they had gone through. When the boys in the group talk about their own victimization, the therapist uses the opportunity to help them empathize with what pain they caused in their victim.

. . . .

These case examples from the therapy of juvenile sex offenders illustrate some of the typical issues: the secrecy, the abuse that often goes on from one generation to the next, and the strange blindness exhibited by the adults with regard to sexual exploitation. The cases also exemplify the flexibility, commitment, and resourcefulness necessary to work with these families. They reflect the basic premise of a therapy of social action: that people can change when guided by a therapist who is clear about what is morally right and who believes that self-determination is possible. All the juvenile sex offenders took responsibility for their actions, apologized to their families, and did reparation. They all understood that they had the power to choose what their future would be, even in spite of great social difficulties. Unfortunately, some of these difficulties stem from the court system. In Chapter Eight we will look at some of the ways in which the courts can interfere with the prevention of violence.

When a juvenile offender does not undergo successful treatment, the chances are very great that he will molest hundreds of children in the course of his life and that he will be violent in ways other than sexual. One of these forms of violence is wife abuse, the subject of the next chapter.

7

Abusive Husbands

T he first task for the therapist when facing a problem of marital violence is to determine when a situation is dangerous. How to intervene will depend on the severity of the situation. One must take into consideration the history of violence in each of the spouse's families, what abuse has already occurred, the history of violence toward others, and what risk there is to the children.

Separation

After considering all these factors, if the therapist decides that there is risk of injury, the therapy must begin with a separation between husband and wife. The therapist needs to take responsibility for this separation and insist that the separation take place immediately. One more episode of violence can be devastating to the victim and cannot be risked. It's unrealistic to think that the police or the court will act expeditiously. Neither will do anything until serious abuse has already occurred. It behooves the therapist to take responsibility for the prevention of violence since no one else will do it.

Typically we tell the couple in the first session, after evaluating the situation, that they need to separate, at least for the moment. After the separation, the therapy will proceed and the therapist will decide at what point in time the couple will be ready to live together again. For the moment, living together is too dangerous, so they must separate. Sometimes it's necessary for the wife to obtain a restraining order so the batterer can be arrested if he attempts contact.

This approach was inspired to a great extent by the work of Milton Erickson, who never hesitated to make such decisions. Perhaps today a therapist might be afraid of a malpractice suit when insisting that a couple separate. Erickson had no such fear. He would ask a wife to go home, pack a small suitcase, and leave immediately without letting anyone know where she would be. Even Erickson didn't want to know. A couple of months later she could send him a postcard so he would be reassured that she was safe. Erickson would not hesitate to make this decision if he felt the woman's life was in danger.

Where I differ with Erickson is that I would be careful to hook both husband and wife to significant others at the time that I'm separating them. The danger of violence and suicide is too great if a spouse is left isolated from family and friends. So in a first session, I tell the couple that each must reconnect to their family of origin. Right there from the therapy room, I might call the wife's father (or mother, uncle, grandmother, etc.) and say that I need his help because I'm concerned about the safety of his daughter, that she is in a dangerous situation in her marriage and needs help. I might ask him to pick her up from the session and take her home with him, or to purchase an airline or a bus ticket for her so she can go straight to the airport or bus terminal. If there are children, I will arrange for her to come home to her family with the children.

I will do the same for the husband and perhaps call his mother to say that her job is not done yet, that she has not finished raising him. A violent man is a man who has not grown up. His temper is out of control, and he is a threat to his wife. He needs to come home to his mother, and she has to teach him once more not to be violent.

So before husband and wife leave the session, I have connected them to their families and I am talking to their relatives. I will continue involving the families in different configurations for as long as it takes to make sure that there will be no more violence. Engaging the extended family is the best way to enforce a separation when necessary and to prevent future violence. Even when the relatives live far away, they can be engaged when the situation is life threatening. In the cases when there is no family, I will involve members of the church or the community to perform the duties of family in protecting both the victim and the abuser.

Rituals

A ritual is a symbolic act that signifies a rite of passage or means that the past is set aside and will not be repeated. Rituals can be simple, such as a birthday party, a visit to relatives, or a renewal of marital vows. They can also involve several complicated steps. What is important is for the drama of the ritual to match the severity of the presenting problem.

In a case where a husband had been physically abusive to the wife over a long period of time and the wife had attempted to murder him, the therapist used two rituals (among many other interventions). First, he asked each spouse to give him their wedding rings, which he would not return to them until he believed that they could once again be truly married.

Then he asked them to cut off all their hair, leaving only half an inch of hair on their heads. The hair that they cut was to be put jointly in a jar and, with this jar, they would drive up a mountain in Virginia where George Washington used to take Martha when he was courting her. At the top of the mountain, they would find a tree where George and Martha used to sit. Under this tree, they would dig a hole in the ground and, in this hole, bury the jar of hair. With this hair their past would be buried, with all the horrible things that they had done to one another, which they would never do again. Yet the past must always be remembered so it will not be repeated. They would always know where the hair was, and, when they needed to remember, they could go back up the mountain and under the tree to think about the terrible things they had done to one another that they would never do again.

One might think that to ask people to cut off their hair as a therapeutic ritual is too extreme. However, it is barely symbolic of the acts of aggression that the spouses had inflicted on each other. When people are so extreme as to attempt murder, the therapist's directives must also be extreme or they won't even be heard.

Creating a Calm Atmosphere

One of the problems in working with marital violence is that spouses can start fighting in a session, making therapy impossible. The therapist needs to frame the situation from the beginning in such a way that the session can be conducted in an atmosphere conducive to peaceful interactions. There are different ways of doing this.

One way is to prevent the spouses from talking to each other and only permit them to address the therapist and respond to the therapist. That is, the therapist becomes the central person in the sessions, and all communication must go through her. Another way is to explicitly state that if voices rise or insults are interchanged, the session will have to be interrupted.

An indirect way is perhaps most powerful in difficult situations. In planning the supervision of the couple mentioned previously who were asked to cut off their hair, I discussed with Neil Schiff, the therapist, how we could create a calm context with a couple who was so violent. Neil was worried about even being able to conduct a conversation with them. I suggested that there was a way, but I said I wasn't sure that Neil was brave enough to do it. He said he certainly was, so I told him my plan.

As soon as the couple came into the therapy room for the first session, before talking about anything else, Neil said, "I must tell you a couple of things before we start. One is that I'm an anxious person." He swallowed after saying this. "I feel very uptight some-times when there's a lot of pressure in a situation, particularly if peo-ple yell at each other and so forth. I find that I can't do very much. I just go blank, if you know what I mean. . . . So if that's something that's likely to happen here, you'll probably see me . . . and I feel that I should tell you this now so you're prepared . . . because it's not the kind of handicap that you can just see. . . . You'll probably see my eyes glaze a little bit, and I'll start to swallow in an awkward kind of way. If that happens, we'll just have to stop for a minute and let things calm down a bit, because otherwise I won't be able to help you very much. I just can't, you know . . . I just can't. . . . You know how some people just can't stand heights? I just can't . . . ahh, . . . I just fall apart when things get real tense. . . . OK?"

The wife said, "You mean if things get real tense between us and we start yelling at each other?"

"Probably you'll have to stop to pick me up," said Neil, "because I will lose it myself. You'll probably see that, but I just wanted to let you know so that if I started to have a funny look and swallow in an odd way, you'd know, and you'd stop what you were doing to lend me a hand. Then later we could go back to what we were doing."

From that session on, the spouses were very careful not to raise their voices or fight with each other. They were very considerate of Neil and seemed to always be looking at him to see how he was feel-ing. This approach seems manipulative, but in fact it wasn't. Neil was truly afraid of the couple's violence. He had never worked before with someone who had attempted murder, and he was truly afraid of not being able to control the sessions. This technique of the explicitly "shy and nervous therapist," is sometimes helpful in bringing out the best in people so that therapy can take place.

Orienting Toward the Future

Violence is often associated with a sordid outlook on life. A man can lose his temper over any sordid, trivial detail of domesticity and fail to see the broader picture in terms of goals, priorities, and the meaning of life. The person is focused on negativity and forgets about the pursuit of happiness. When one has lost perspective on the course of one's life, violent tantrums seem an appropriate response to minor inconveniences. Family life becomes a nightmare.

This was the situation of a couple who came to therapy with a serious problem. The wife was severely diabetic and was drinking herself to death. She drank a half bottle of vodka a night and was not paying attention to her diet or her medications. She said it was the husband's violence that drove her to drink.

The husband was a very tall, big man who had violent temper tantrums. While having dinner with his wife and three children, he would on occasion take a plate of spaghetti and smash it against the wall. He would push the wife and make her fall, or squeeze her arm too hard. He was so big that his mere presence could be threatening. He just had to move in a certain way and there was the implication of violence.

I was the supervisor in the case, and the therapist, Stephen Williams, was very formal and polite, always dressed in a suit and tie. There was a big contrast between the way he and the husband presented themselves, and an even bigger contrast with the wife, who was a tall, bloated woman who came to the sessions wearing shorts and curlers in her hair. The couple talked endlessly about messes: the attic, the garage, cleaning up after the dog, taking out the garbage.

No matter what we tried, the tension between the spouses didn't improve, the conversation always went back to the sordid and menial, and there was always the threat of violence. I could see that the couple was not improving, and the therapist was definitely worse. He seemed more and more depressed. I could see that he was thinking, "For this I struggled through a Ph.D." I had to do something not just to help the couple but to help the therapist.

One day I said to Steve when we were planning the session behind the one-way mirror, "Today I would like you to do something unusual. Go in and ask the wife whether she has seen the movie or read the book *Gone with the Wind.* She is going to say 'Why are you asking?' Tell her it's because she and her husband remind you so much of Rhett Butler and Scarlet O'Hara. They also had a passionate relationship, always fighting. Like Rhett, her husband is always on the edge of violence; Scarlet was always trying to change him, but she never succeeded—she never changed him at all."

As soon as the therapist went into the therapy room and made this statement, the husband looked at himself in the mirror. The only resemblance he had to Clark Gable was his mustache, and he started to stroke it, smiling to himself. The wife said, "*Gone with the Wind* is my favorite novel! I've read the book four times. I've seen the movie probably six times! And Scarlet did change Rhett!"

The therapist said, "No, she didn't. I'll bet you $10 that you won't find a passage in the book that shows that she changed him. I'm surprised that knowing the novel so well, you think you can succeed where Scarlet failed, and you keep trying to change your husband instead of enjoying his unpredictability and the passionate relationship you have with him."

The wife said she would read the book again and find the places where it's clear that Scarlet did change Rhett. Later she admitted she had lost the bet. Rhett had never actually changed. But the conversation about *Gone with the Wind* had already set the context for a different type of interaction. The spouses were identifying with the prototypical romantic, passionate couple. The therapist had momentarily raised them to a higher level of being.

Then the therapist proceeded to ask, "I'd like you to tell me what are the best memories of your life together? Way back in the past when you first met, what were the best times that you had together?"

At first they couldn't think of any good memories at all. But the therapist insisted: "There must have been some good times. Perhaps your honeymoon, the birth of the first child. . . ."

Slowly they began to remember. The husband told how they

went on their honeymoon to a place in Florida where there was a dolphin show. One evening he went by himself for a walk and saw the trainer practicing with the dolphins. He learned the signals that the trainer gave to the dolphins for the show. The next day he took his wife to the lagoon, gave the dolphins the signals, and they jumped out of the water putting on a show just for her. Listening to this, the therapist began to get interested in the man. He was more imaginative than the therapist had thought. The wife softened as she remembered the episode.

Then they remembered a couple of other charming incidents in their lives. The therapist told them that in the next two weeks he wanted them to just do one thing, and that was to create one good memory that would be remembered ten years from now, like the episode with the dolphins. Who did the dishes, who took out the garbage, who cleaned the attic, was not going to be remembered ten years from now. But an unusual event, a special memory, would be something that would be theirs always to treasure.

That day was the first snow of the winter. When they left the session, the husband built an enormous snowman right at the door of our institute. The snowman lasted a long time and it is a memory that I always treasure.

For two months the therapy continued with the only directive, every other week, of creating another good memory. All conversation about violence, the couple's relationship, and the wife's diabetes were abandoned, except as it related to the good memories they were creating. They discovered wonderful things to do for free with each other and with their children. As they created good memories, the wife's health improved; she quit drinking and began to take care of her diabetes. After three months there was no longer a problem for therapy.

To solve problems of violence, one cannot only focus on the violence. It's necessary to raise people to a higher level where they can envision a better way of being.

Fines and Contracts

One way to stop a man's violence is to set up consequences for the violence such that the consequences are so detrimental that they cannot compensate for the satisfaction of exerting violence. If a man is violent, it is because he derives an advantage or satisfaction from the violence. If, instead, he derives a penalty, he may stop being violent.

I don't believe in impulses out of control. There is always some offer that the violent person can't refuse. So either you can pay a man for not being violent, or you can make him pay if he is violent. Paying him for not being violent is not often feasible, but making him pay if he is, is usually possible.

Establishing a contract for such a fine can be as follows:

1. Typically when the couple comes to therapy, the victim is the one who wants to solve the problem. The husband usually doesn't see that there is a problem and doesn't even want to come to therapy. So the first step is to find a motivation for the violent spouse to want to change and stop the violence. The therapist needs to talk to the husband about how painful it must be to hurt someone one loves, to hurt the woman who is the mother of one's children, to give fear to the children because they see their mother hurt.

   The therapist explains that she has the husband's best interest at heart and is worried about the consequences for him, in terms of jeopardizing his position in the community as a respectable person and a law-abiding citizen, emphasizing that the most serious consequences, if the violence doesn't stop, will be for the husband, who will suffer a loss of dignity, self-respect, and the respect of his children.

2. The second step is that the therapist says that there is a way to stop the violence. If the husband follows the therapist's

suggestions, it's absolutely guaranteed that there will be no more violence. That is, what the therapist wants to propose is like buying insurance against violence.

3. Once the husband says that he wants to hear the therapist's proposal, the therapist explains that it involves a contract of sorts. The husband is to open a bank account in the name of his mother-in-law (or the wife's children from a previous marriage, or the wife's brother, anyone the husband is not particularly fond of). In this account, he is to deposit a certain amount of money. The amount should be commensurate to the husband's situation. It could be $100 or $20,000. Whatever the amount, it should be substantial for that particular man, so that its loss will hurt. Should the man ever hit his wife again, the money will automatically go to his mother-in-law (or whoever else was assigned) to do with it what she wants. Then the account will be reestablished for double the amount of money, and the same consequence will apply should he hit his wife again.

4. The therapist needs to be prepared for the fact that the husband will not immediately accept this contract. Typically, he will say that it's not fair and doesn't even address the problem. The problem is the wife's provocation. He hits her because she provokes him. If she didn't provoke him, he wouldn't hit her. The therapist can say that the law punishes violence; it doesn't punish provocation. The husband should not resort to violence no matter what the provocation. However, since it's conceivable that the wife might think, "My mother needs some money—I'll provoke him a little," the therapist can propose a modification of the contract. Should the husband hit the wife and in his judgment it's a result of her provocation, then the money goes to a charity, instead of to the mother-in-law. And it should be a charity different from any that he

might usually contribute to. A violent husband may not ordinarily give money to any charity, so the loss will hurt him almost as much as if it went to his mother-in-law.

5. When the therapist talks about the issue of provocation, the husband usually becomes very hostile against the therapist, even to the point of threatening him. It doesn't matter whether the therapist is a man or a woman, young or old, experienced or inexperienced. The therapist must respond to this threat with kindness and tolerance. It's very important to model for the husband that it's possible to respond to provocation other than with hostility. The therapist needs to emphasize once again that she has the husband's best interest at heart and wants to help him have a better life. This is a time when a long speech by the therapist, in a low hypnotic voice, is useful toward diffusing hostility.

6. The therapist needs to be prepared for the fact that the husband will not accept the contract until it has been renegotiated and he feels he has gained an advantage. The husband will typically say that the amount of money is excessive, that it should be less, or that the wife should contribute to the fund. In anticipation of this renegotiation, the therapist has to begin with a higher price than he is willing to settle for. So, at this point, the therapist can agree with the husband and reduce the amount of money in half or accept that the wife will contribute half of the amount.

   It's very important to be prepared for the renegotiation, because a violent husband always has to feel that he has somehow won, that he was smarter than the therapist; and it's alright to let him feel that. Whatever is agreed on, the point is that the next time the husband is tempted to hit, he will know that one punch will cost him X amount of money that he would rather not spend in this way.

7. A stipulation in the contract can be that, if at the end of one year, the husband has not hit the wife, they will use the money to have a pleasant time together, such as a party or a vacation.

This strategy is guaranteed. If the price is high enough, and if the therapist sets up the bank account so that the consequence will be enforced, the husband will not hit the wife again.

Third Parties

Probably the most important strategy in preventing marital violence is to involve a third person in the marriage. For marital violence to take place it has to be private and secret. In the presence of another adult, the violence will stop. This strategy is particularly useful when a separation between the spouses cannot be arranged, or when the violence continues even after the couple is separated.

The therapist can ask a relative or a friend to come to stay at the couple's home or, if the couple is already separated, to stay with one of the spouses, never leaving his or her side to ensure that there is no more violence. For example, sometimes a couple is living separately, but the husband frequently appears at the wife's home to quarrel with her and beat her. The therapist can speak to the husband's mother, explain to her the danger in the situation, and ask her to move in with her son and follow him around constantly to make sure he will not be violent again. If the couple is still living together, the mother can actually move into the house with them. The therapist must explain to her that she has to prevent her son from ending in jail even if it means that she has to follow him around and bother him constantly.

When a third person is introduced, even if it is temporarily, it's possible to have some calm and, without the constant threat of violence, the therapist can focus on other strategies for a permanent solution without the constant presence of the third party.

The Steps

The method described for working with sex offenders can be adapted to the therapy of violent husbands. Here are the recommended steps:

Step 1. The therapist meets with the couple and their parents and siblings, bringing together as many older adults in the family as possible, and asks the couple to tell everyone about all the episodes of violence. In a therapy of social action, a goal is to reorganize the natural family network so that checks and balances are established to prevent further abuse. The violent person must take responsibility for how his actions affect not only the victim but the whole family.

Step 2. The therapist asks the husband why it was wrong to hit his wife. Often the husband has trouble accepting that it was wrong and, instead, attempts to justify his violence by bringing up issues of provocation. The therapist asks the other adults to help him understand that he is the only person responsible for his own violence, and why it was wrong. Sometimes the other family members have trouble understanding, perhaps because there are other victims and abusers in the family. But the therapist must persist until the abuser takes full responsibility for his actions and understands the pain and humiliation of the victim.

Step 3. The therapist explains the spiritual pain of being abused by the person one trusts most: one's husband and the father of one's children.

Step 4. The therapist asks the husband to get on the floor on his knees to express his sorrow and repentance for having abused the wife, taking full responsibility for what he did and promising never to do it again. The family and the therapist have to judge that the apology is sincere, or he has to do it over and over again until everyone agrees he is sincere.

Step 5. The family then discusses what the consequences will be should the husband ever hit the wife again, and the therapist encourages them to agree on consequences such as pressing charges against the husband and enforcing a separation between the spouses.

Step 6. The family chooses a protector for the victim, someone who will stay involved and watch her closely to make sure she is alright. The protector might even have to move in temporarily with the victim, or the victim with the protector.

Step 7. The family can decide on an act of reparation that the husband is to do for the wife to demonstrate his repentance and his love.

After these steps, the therapy can proceed with the therapist sometimes meeting alone with the couple to help them negotiate their differences and sometimes with the whole family until there is no longer a threat of violence.

Fred and Ginger

Ginger was referred to me by her stepfather, who was a professor at a local university. She said she had a problem of violence in her marriage and had moved in with her mother and stepfather, who had insisted that she come to therapy with me.

Ginger came to the first session alone with her three-month-old baby. She was a beautiful young woman with long, straight, blonde hair and a look of devotion for her baby, whom she nursed almost continuously. She said there had been a great deal of tension in the marriage because her husband, Fred, had emigrated from Europe and was having difficulty keeping a steady job. He had given up his career in Europe because she wanted to be close to her family, and now they found they were very poor and her family wasn't helping them.

She told me that Fred had started to hit her in Europe, right after she got pregnant. She said it wasn't very bad; he just punched her in the arm or slapped her on the face. I suspected she was minimizing the violence, like many abused women.

I told Ginger I needed to meet with her husband and with as many people in her family as could be brought together. She said that she didn't want to tell her father for fear of upsetting him too much. I promised I would protect her father from getting too upset but insisted that he should come. I asked her whether I should call each family member or whether there was a central person that I could talk to who would bring them all in. She said that if I spoke with her mother, she would bring everyone in.

Present at the second session were Fred and Ginger, her mother and stepfather, her father and stepmother, two brothers, and a sister. I said I had invited them to come to help me put an end to Fred's violence against Ginger and with the goal of bringing the young couple back together as a family again. The mother and stepfather both said that they would like to see them back together, but, given the violence, they didn't know if that would be realistic.

I asked each person in the family to tell me everything they knew about the violence, and, as the mother and the stepmother talked, I realized that it was much more serious than what Ginger had described. The mother had taken Ginger to the hospital for loss of hearing in one ear as a consequence of being hit on the head. Fred had locked her up in their apartment on numerous occasions and hit her for hours at a time. The brothers and sister and the father were shocked and furious to hear all this.

I turned to Fred, who sat very formally dressed in a suit, lovingly holding the baby on his lap, tall, gaunt, and dark—totally in contrast to Ginger who sat beside him. He said he missed his wife and his baby and wanted them to come home. I asked him why his violence was wrong. With a heavy accent, he answered that violence is bad, it hurts, but I should understand that Ginger has a terrible personality and provoked him to violence.

I explained how provocation was not an excuse and asked the family to support my view. We went around the circle again, and once more I asked Fred why his violence was wrong. He said he had had meningitis as a child and believed that, as a consequence, he had some brain damage that caused him to lose control. The step-father supported this view, saying that perhaps Fred should be on medication. I asked Fred how many people he had beaten up. He said he had never hit anyone.

I asked again if he had hit a former girlfriend, perhaps someone at work, or someone in his family. He said he had never been violent with anyone except Ginger. I said that was very interesting. I had never heard of a brain damage that is specific to abusing your wife and your wife alone. Everyone saw my point and agreed that the violence could not be the result of a neurological problem.

So I asked him once more why it was wrong to hit his wife. He said it was wrong because he loved her and she was the mother of his child, but she did provoke him. This conversation went on for more than half an hour until he accepted that his violence was wrong no matter what the provocation from Ginger.

I explained the spiritual pain that his abuse had caused in Ginger: to be attacked by her husband whom she loved and trusted, the father of her child; to be nursing the baby to whom her chemical reaction of fear was being transmitted; to be not just hit but tortured systematically for long periods of time. Fred said he understood.

So I asked him to get on his knees in front of Ginger and express his sorrow and repentance for having abused her. He said he wanted to apologize, but he wouldn't get on his knees. The issue was not his apology, he said. I had to help them get along better. I had to change Ginger's obnoxious personality.

I said I could only do that after I saw him take full responsibility for his violence and demonstrate true sorrow and repentance, for which he needed to get on his knees and apologize to Ginger. He said he wouldn't get on his knees.

I asked the family's help and one by one they talked to him. The brothers said they wanted to kill him. I asked them to be calm and expressed how much I appreciated their presence, since they were close in age to Fred and their advice was particularly important. The father talked about his own pain at being betrayed by Fred whom he had trusted and helped. Several times Fred turned to Ginger and said that he was sorry. He cried so much that one could see the tears falling on the carpet, but he wouldn't get on his knees.

I said that if the family didn't feel that Fred was truly repentant and there would be no more violence, they could not let Ginger come home. Everyone agreed and said they saw no signs that Fred would change. I insisted that he should get on his knees.

After more than half an hour like this, I asked the women to leave the room. Wife abuse is a problem of men, and I said I wanted the men in the family to talk to Fred. We went around the circle again, and the men talked about taking responsibility for one's actions, about not thinking of a woman as property, about the love for one's child. The brothers, who were big and strong, explained what they did to control their temper. It was to no avail. Fred wouldn't get on his knees. I asked the men what they would do if Fred ever hit Ginger again, and they said they would report him to the police and he would be immediately deported.

Finally, I ended the session saying that we would have to meet again as a whole family the following week. Until Fred apologized appropriately I couldn't continue with the rest of the therapy. In the meantime, Ginger would live with her mother and stepfather. It was agreed that Fred could visit her and the baby at the parents' home.

At the beginning of the next session, without further pressure, Fred got on his knees and apologized. Again he was crying profusely, and he expressed his sorrow and repentance sincerely, to the family's satisfaction. He promised he would never hit Ginger again. He wanted her to come home.

I felt that after the apology in front of the family, plus the threat of the brothers' violence and the threat of deportation, Fred would not hit Ginger again. But the family thought differently. They didn't want Ginger to go home and were even afraid for the baby's safety. I respected their view. It was decided that the brothers would be Ginger's special protectors. Another month went by until Ginger and the baby went back to the apartment with Fred.

In the meantime, we continued to have family sessions dealing with issues of money, Fred's work, and Ginger's demands and bad temper.

The problem with money was that there was not enough but they liked to live very well. They were both always fashionably dressed, and they loved to eat well, especially Fred who was the cook of the two.

Meanwhile, Fred was working in a job that was beneath his abilities and was also facing all the difficulties of being a foreigner. He came home frustrated and anxious about the future. One of the problems at work was that Ginger would call him on the phone to bicker or just to talk and would never hang up, so we arranged that a phone call at work could not take more than five minutes.

Ginger did have a bad temper. She was extremely uncooperative in terms of doing anything that Fred wanted, unless it was precisely what she herself wanted to do. For example, in the evening she would sit and read a book. If Fred asked her a question, she would refuse to answer because she was engrossed in the book. She liked to read in silence, refusing to engage with him for hours. This was extraordinarily frustrating to Fred, who liked to come home and have conversations.

I suggested that any time Ginger exhibited bad temper, the consequence would be that she would cook the next dinner instead of Fred. Fred said that would be a punishment for him—he preferred to suffer her bad temper rather than her bad cooking. So we negotiated other consequences.

The couple stabilized in a more normal relationship even though they continued to have money problems. After a year since the beginning of therapy, there has been no more violence.

Negotiating Differences

Once the threat of violence has disappeared, the therapist needs to focus on helping the couple negotiate their differences without hostility. One way of doing this is by coaching them to have "win-win" negotiations—that is, negotiations that end with both parties happy with their agreement. By contrast, a "win-lose" negotiation is one that ends with the couple having the perception that one spouse "won" and one "lost." Sometimes a spouse will have so many experiences of "losing" that he or she will not be willing to negotiate at all, so the therapist must clearly explain that she will arrange for a win-win situation.

Some negotiations in marriage are explicit. The exchange is defined and clear. Each partner knows exactly what each is getting and what each is giving. For example, one spouse agrees to move to another city in exchange for the other agreeing to change careers. An implicit negotiation is one where one partner agrees to a request by the other without explicitly asking for something in return. For example, one spouse may ask the other to change the daily routine and cook dinner. The other spouse might agree without asking for something in return, and yet expect something in return. Always the party that concedes to a request is expecting something in return. All requests in marriage are quid pro quos. Something is given in return for something.

Most negotiations between spouses are implicit. When implicit negotiations break down, it is necessary for the couple to take on an explicit style of negotiation. The following are steps, developed by Jim Keim, for a win-win negotiation in therapy.

Step 1. Each spouse is asked to write down a list of items to be negotiated, a "want" list. The list must include at least one item that has to do with fun and entertainment.

Step 2. The negotiation process will start with the item of having fun as a couple. For example, if the wife has on her list that she wants to go dancing and the husband has on his that he wants to go to the movies, this is the first item that they will negotiate.

Step 3.   The therapist explains that this negotiation is only the first of many. Since there are going to be many more, it is important to start with the spouses enjoying each other's company, so that future negotiations can proceed in a friendly, happy atmosphere. This is why good business negotiators often entertain those they plan to do business with. This is why Japanese businessmen, who are well-known for their excellent negotiation strategies, always end negotiations with a long, friendly dinner.

Step 4.   The therapist explains the rules for negotiating:

1. Never say no. The closest one can come to no is saying, "I will think about it."

2. Only the present and the future can be negotiated. Avoid bringing up the past except as an example of what is being requested.

3. Assume that one knows only what is best for oneself and not for the other. Questioning the validity of the other's request is perceived as hostile or patronizing.

4. Each partner owes the other a "price" in exchange for the request that is being negotiated.

5. Be very specific about the terms of your request. For example, negotiate for time segments of only one week at a time. Describe a request in behavioral terms. "Be more loving" is too general. "Hug me once a day" is appropriately specific. Break requests into simple behaviors.

6. Hold hands during negotiations. It's very difficult to quarrel with someone when you are holding her hand.

7. Seal all negotiations with a kiss.

8. Do not end a negotiation until each partner feels that a win-win situation exists, so that each is happy with the negotiated agreement. Write down the agreement.

Step 5. When the first negotiation has been completed, move on to another item. Continue negotiating like this during several sessions. The therapist shouldn't let the couple negotiate out of the therapy room until several successful negotiations have been completed in the sessions.

. . . .

The strategies and steps that I described in this chapter are not contradictory with each other and can be used sequentially in a therapy of marital violence. They are all part of a therapy of social action based on an interactional view.

We are not products of our childhood experiences. We have the power to choose—the power of self-determination. If current interactions change, the individual will change. The extended family—the natural tribe—is an important part of an individual's current interactions. When the relatives organize to prevent violence, abuse will stop. A responsible therapist will guide a family to take responsibility for its members, so that each individual will in turn be responsible for his own actions and violence will be prevented.

8

Judges' and Therapists' Mistakes

The most common mistake made by therapists in cases of family violence is not to collaborate closely with the courts. We have to educate the court system as to what we need from them and what they can expect from us. We must be very clear about what is right and wrong, and we must stand up for our clients to defend their rights. We must protest a punishment that is too severe or a court order that interferes with the therapy or that is not in the best interest of the child. Even though we are not expected to contribute unless we are asked to testify, we must make ourselves heard. The court can be equally or more abusive than the family. Just as we sometimes have to protect children from their parents, so we have to protect children and adults from the courts.

The most common mistake made by judges is to send people to jail instead of court-ordering family therapy, probation, and community service. A person should be institutionalized only when the therapist gives up and cannot control the violence. Therapy is cheaper than jail. It's not a place where one can learn bad things from other inmates. And in family therapy, several people can benefit.

Another typical mistake that judges make is not listening to the children and failing to understand that it is a human right of children to be close to their mother, even if the mother is not the best person in the world. Too often children are separated from their mother when it is the father who presents the problem.

The following case studies illustrate some of the difficulties in court-involved cases.

Attempted Murder

Rhonda called the Family Therapy Institute to initiate therapy. She and her husband, David, had been divorced for a year. Rhonda initially had custody of their two children: a six-year-old boy and a four-year-old girl. Six months following the initial decision that gave the mother custody, the father resumed his attempts to gain custody of the children. He found a therapist who substantiated some of his feelings that it wasn't the best arrangement for the mother to have primary custody of the children, basically because she had a boyfriend who had some prior criminal history. He had been charged once in the past with disorderly conduct, and he had threatened the husband with physical harm because he kept interfering with the wife's new life.

David had a prestigious, stable, intellectual job and no previous history of violence. He spent almost his life's savings on lawyers to regain custody of the children. In the hearing, the judge overturned the original custody arrangement, and the children then moved in with the father, who hired a housekeeper to help him.

The children had been very happy living with their mother and liked her boyfriend. They had not been involved in the court hearing. The judge had never asked them where they preferred to live.

A month later, the boy, Randy, set the father's house on fire. He said he had been playing with matches on his sister's bed, but everyone in the family believed that he had set the fire deliberately. The whole top of the house was burned down, but everyone escaped without injury.

The mother initiated therapy after the fire because the children were very upset. The father had agreed that they move in temporarily with the mother because the house was unlivable. The repairs would take three or four months since the damage was severe. David moved into an apartment. He was in his fifties, and this was his second divorce. He was an only child, and his parents were dead. Rhonda was twenty years younger than David. She was also very gifted in her profession. Both parents were very involved in cultural activities with the children.

At the initiation of therapy, both parents agreed that they had to learn to get along with each other and stop causing pain to the children, who were very distraught over Mom and Dad's behavior. The parents had terrible fights when the father accused the mother for being with this terrible man. He would call her names in front of the children, upsetting them greatly. The mother was very devoted to the children and truly enjoyed playing with them. This had been used against her in court where the previous psychologist had suggested that she was almost adolescent in her interests and more a playmate than a parent. The family therapist never found her to be like that at all. She was a very adequate parent who knew how to relate to the children very well.

When they first came to therapy, the children were upset because of the fire and because of Mom and Dad's fighting. They were happy to be back with their mother, who saw this situation as an opportunity to regain custody. Neither parent wanted joint custody because they couldn't work together. The therapy plan was to work with the parents periodically but also to work with the children on some of their fears and anxieties and help them cope with the parents' divorce.

Every time the parents came to a session they would fight. The father was very angry that the mother had left him. He didn't want to be a single parent and refused to be a part-time parent. He couldn't be led to reason about the situation and was so angry that he actually foamed at the mouth. The therapist saw David alone a couple of times to try to hear his side of the story so he could vent his anger and frustration. She sympathized with some of his feelings. She couldn't influence him, however, and he continued to be irrational whenever he talked with his ex-wife. David had never been physically violent, but he had often engaged in intense quarrels over little things. For example, he would get into arguments with neighbors about the property and then he would throw lit cigarette butts into the neighbors' cars.

In therapy, Randy was very afraid of saying anything critical of his dad, but he would draw pictures expressing that he wanted to harm his father. The therapist thought the reason was that the father said bad things to Randy about his mother, yet she couldn't stop the father from doing this. David understood that it was wrong, but he couldn't control himself. It was as if he constantly needed to obsess out loud against his ex-wife. He even told Randy that when his mother became pregnant with him, she had wanted to have an abortion, and that in fact she had aborted another pregnancy after Randy was born. This was a terrible thing to say to a six-year-old.

After four months of therapy, the father was getting very upset because he saw how the mother was trying to build a case to regain custody of the children. When the repairs on the house were finished, David wanted the children back, but Rhonda said it would disrupt them to move when they were just beginning to do well. The school had given good reports, and Randy had not set any more fires. In a session with the parents alone, the mother explained that the children wanted to live with her but were afraid of saying this to the father. He agreed not to ask them any more about where they preferred to live. Both parents agreed that the therapist would talk to the children, and both would accept her decision about what would be best for them.

When the therapist asked Randy how he would feel if he went back to live with Dad, Randy drew a picture of a house with smoke coming out of the top floor and a stick figure with a smoking gun in his hand. He said that if he had to live with Dad, he would have to shoot him.

The therapist met with the parents and said that she thought that Randy should continue to live with his mother. David became very angry at her and said he would take the matter to court. Rhonda said she would go to court to seek custody.

After that session, David took the children on a vacation, and, when they returned, he took them out of therapy. Once again, he hired a psychologist to testify in his favor.

The therapist was subpoenaed to testify about the therapy. She related what the children had said and presented the judge with Randy's drawing. The expert witness hired by the father refuted her testimony, saying that the child's drawing had no bearing on the case. The judge dismissed the psychologist, saying that because the psychologist was so biased in favor of the father, the judge would never allow him to testify again in his courtroom.

The judge then ordered a home study to be conducted by a court-appointed psychologist and social worker. There was another hearing three months later, where the judge gave custody to the mother and spoke angrily to the father about his inappropriate behavior with the children. Also, because the school had been such a stabilizing influence in the children's lives, the judge ordered the father out of the house where he was living and the mother to move into that house with the children so they could be closer to school. Everyone, even Rhonda, thought this wasn't a good idea. From David's point of view, he lost not only his children but also his house. He also now had no money because he had lost it all in lawyer's fees.

Three weeks later, a few days before Christmas, David went to his house, which was now Rhonda's house, with the intent to kill her. She was at a Christmas party, and the children were at their grandmother's. David got into the house somehow. Rhonda's boyfriend, Bob, was living there. He came down the stairs, thinking that Rhonda had come home, and David shot him twice, in the lungs and in the back. Then David ran upstairs looking for Rhonda, then came back down the stairs while Bob pretended to be dead. David then went through the mail and finally walked out on the street where he ranted and raved to passers-by, scaring a neighbor's child with questions about Rhonda and the children. In the meantime, Bob dragged himself to the phone and called the police. David was immediately arrested and never released on bond.

David was charged with attempted murder, and assault and bat-tery, but the jury found him guilty only of the lesser charge. The judge was upset at this decision but could only give a ten-year sen-tence of which four years were suspended.

A few months after the trial, Rhonda married Bob, who is now disabled from the wounds. She promised to let the therapist know when David comes out of jail. David made threats not only against the therapist but also against the two professionals who made the home study.

· · · · · · ·

How could this whole sequence of events have been avoided? Prob-ably the first big mistake was made by the first judge who gave David custody of the children. Otherwise he might have adapted to the divorce and to visitation. Once he had been awarded custody, David felt justified in his anger at Rhonda for attempting to take the chil-dren away from him. When the children are so young and so con-nected to the mother, and the mother is adequate, the judge should give custody to the mother and order the whole family to therapy so the parents can work out difficulties over visitation.

The second mistake by the judge was to order David out of his house in favor of Rhonda and the children. If David had kept his house, if the judge had given him liberal visitation, or even joint custody, and had court-ordered the family to therapy so that once or twice a week the difficulties between mother and father would be negotiated, perhaps the tragedy would have been avoided.

A Loaf of Bread

A seventeen-year-old boy, Mario, had been charged with two sep-arate attempted rapes of two teenage girls. He lived with his mother, stepfather, and a younger brother. He was very addicted to alcohol. The court sent him first to an alcohol treatment center to detoxify and then he was going to be placed in a juvenile jail. The mother, however, insisted that she wanted Mario to have another opportunity to live at home, so the court decided to electronically monitor him at home, to continue the urine screening to make sure he was free of drugs and alcohol, and to refer him to our institute for therapy in regard to the sex offenses he had committed.

Mario had attempted suicide prior to the alcohol treatment. He carved on himself and had numerous scars on his body, presenting not only suicidal ideation but very self-destructive behavior. The therapy involved Mario's mother and brother. The therapist was unable to get the stepfather to come to a session.

Mario had been very violently abused by his biological father, who had also abused the mother. The stepfather had also abused both boys and the mother. It was difficult for Mario to describe the abuse, but the mother explained to the therapist that there had been belts, rods and other instruments used by the biological father, and later fistfights with the stepfather. The family had been involved over many years with Protective Services.

The boys were closer to the stepfather than they had ever been to the biological father. Mario longed to be involved with his biological father, a construction worker, and, while he was in therapy, would frequently spend a day helping him at work. Those visits would often end in an argument, and then he wouldn't see the father again for a long time. Mario had become very belligerent toward his mother as he had gotten older, to the point where she was afraid to set any limits for fear that he would hit her, though he never did.

The first attempted rape had been of a girl he knew in his apartment building who had come to visit him when his mother was away. They were in his bedroom, and he had seduced her into foreplay but then became insistent on intercourse even though the girl was refusing. The second incident involved Mario's girlfriend who was also visiting his room, with the door closed, while the mother was in the apartment. The mother heard noises and tried to go into the room but was unable to do so, while Mario continued to attempt intercourse. In both cases, the girls had pressed charges. Mario plead "involved" in court, although he thought that the girls really wanted to have sex and couldn't understand that they were saying no.

There was a no-contact order, so he couldn't apologize to the girls in person, but once he understood what he had done wrong, the therapist had him write letters of apology that some day he might be able to give them. And Mario did apologize sincerely to his mother and brother for the shame and anguish he had caused them.

During the therapy, Mario became involved with another young woman and became a father. It was an unstable relationship, but the young woman came with him to several sessions. At that time, Mario was doing very well. His urine was clean, he went regularly to AA, and he had a job to pay for the therapy and electronic monitor. So eventually the judge agreed that he could be taken off the electronic monitor. At that point, Mario was eighteen. He moved in with his girlfriend and the baby. He was attending high school with the goal of passing the high school equivalency test.

A few months later, Mario was arrested for stealing a radio from a car. He was on probation until age twenty-one from the previous charges, so if he committed any crime, he could be sent immediately to jail without further process. The judge decided to do precisely that and sent him to jail, ending the therapy abruptly and without further contact with the therapist. He had stolen the radio because he had lost his job and needed money.

The therapy had lasted seven months. Instead of throwing Mario in jail, the judge could have put him back on the electronic monitor, court-ordered him to therapy, and made him do community service. Instead, putting him in jail for stealing a radio from a car, without injury to anyone, was not very different from the medieval punishment of cutting off a hand for stealing a loaf of bread.

Also, Mario wasn't sent to jail for stealing the radio. He was jailed because he had previous charges of attempted rape. Yet, he had never actually raped anyone and had only tried to force himself on girls his age who had voluntarily gone into his bedroom and locked the door. There is such a hysteria over sexual abuse that even judges are losing their common sense about what is a crime and what is simply bad behavior.

The punishment was way too harsh and not conducive to any positive results. People don't change in one jump. For an alcoholic charged with attempted rape, it's a step forward, not a step back, to only steal a car radio in the course of more than one year.

The therapist made the mistake of not fighting for Mario. She should have insisted on being heard by the judge and should have saved him from jail.

· · · · · · ·

The most common mistake made by therapists is not to collaborate closely with referral sources, whoever they may be. When the referral source is an institution such as a hospital, school, or the court system, with power to alter the social context of the individual, this collaboration is crucial. The hospital has the power to institutionalize. The school can expel or segregate a child. The court has the power to imprison. Not to include these forces as part of the therapy is as serious a mistake as not to include the family.

Judges need to be educated to court-order family therapy together with probation and community service. They also have to be reminded to listen to the children and protect their human rights as well as those of mothers. Judges need to understand that people don't change in one jump and therapy is not a cure that ensures that a person will not have a problem again in his life. When there is recidivism and therapy has worked in the past, court-ordered therapy should be enforced once again.

9

The Past

Sometimes a victim of incest and sexual abuse, frightened or sworn to secrecy by the offender, will keep that secret for many years, perhaps for her whole life. Carrying such a secret is demoralizing and isolating. It drains mental energy from the person, and it interferes with current relationships.

The therapist must try by all means to relieve the victim, explaining to her that as long as she carries the secret, she carries the shame. And it is the victimizer who should carry the shame. The longer the secret has been kept, the more difficult it is to reveal it to other family members. Yet this is the only way that the victim can be freed of this burden.

Sometimes an adult will come to therapy with the suspicion that she was molested as a child even though she does not remember. She might request therapy with the goal of recovering a memory of abuse. I think it's appropriate to help people remember, but I don't recommend hypnosis for that purpose. It's too easy to induce false memories under hypnosis. The best way to recover memories is to talk with the family, to see what others in the same or in previous generations remember. Rarely is there only one victim in the family. The chances are that if one child was abused, other children were abused also.

The goal for the therapist is to obtain an apology from the offender for the abuse and from the parents and relatives for not having protected the victim as a child. Everyone who is still alive should come together for an apology session. If the offender or a parent is dead, no one else should role-play their part so as not to take away from the atmosphere of solemnity in which the session should be conducted. The therapist needs to follow as many of the steps for the therapy of offenders and victims as possible, even if the crime occurred thirty years in the past. To accomplish this goal, the first step is to reveal the secret to other family members.

Sometimes the victim gives permission to the therapist to invite everyone in the family to a session where the therapist will reveal the abusive relationship. Parents and other relatives will travel long distances for such a session if the therapist insists on how important it is for the victim. The therapist should say that she needs the family's help and that one session with the family will go a long way in resolving long-standing difficulties.

It would be a mistake to reveal the secret over the phone. This must be done in person so the therapist can control how everyone responds. It is also a mistake to expect the victim to reveal the secret to the family. Usually this is too difficult to do, particularly when the secret has been kept for a long time. The therapist must obtain permission to speak for the victim.

Sometimes it helps to ask the victim to reveal the secret to only one relative and later to another, and so on until everyone knows. Then an apology session can be held with the whole family.

The best argument to convince the victim to reveal the secret is to say that incest and abuse are possible only when they are secret. Research shows that incest runs in families, so chances are that another child in the family is being victimized in the present. The best way to prevent further abuse is to reveal the secret so the children in the family can be protected. A victim may not reveal the secret for her own sake, but she will always do it to protect other children.

The secret of incest can affect future generations of children, even if they are not themselves abused. One of the most moving sessions I have seen involved an eighty-two-year-old woman who consulted us because of her concern about her forty-seven-year-old son, who complained of chronic pain, refused to work, and was homeless. Her other two children were also very disturbed. I thought that to produce three seriously disturbed children, there had to be something horrible in the mother's past. When asked what was the most horrible thing that had happened to her, the old woman related that, at age twelve, her stepfather had used her to simulate intercourse. She had told her mother, who at first protected her from the stepfather but who later turned against her, suspecting that she was having an ongoing sexual relationship with him. She remembered her mother even threatening to burn her face.

When the daughter got married, she insisted on spending the wedding night at her mother's home to prove to her that she was still a virgin. When the mother saw the blood on the sheets, she fell on her knees and apologized to her daughter, but the daughter never forgave her. The three children grew up not understanding why the mother hated the grandmother and with the pain of seeing their loving grandmother mistreated by their loved mother.

When they came to therapy, the woman was eighty-two years old, and all the people in her generation and in the previous generation were dead. So we had a session where she revealed the secret of her abuse and of the conflict with her mother to her children. The therapist asked the homeless son to thank his mother for revealing the secret. Instead of thanking her, he said, "I forgive you for not telling me the secret before." He was right. The secret she kept had hurt her children as well as herself.

Sometimes, no matter what the therapist does, a person can never be sure about what happened in the past and whether or not she was abused as a child. It's best for the therapist to say that so many women and children have suffered terrible abuse over thousands of years that we all carry within us the memory of that pain. Their pain is our pain, so it's not so important to figure out what happened to us as individuals. What's important is to do something to prevent this violence from continuing in future generations. So the therapist directs the person toward a sense of unity and compassion. The best way to overcome trauma is to come out of oneself and help others.

The following case study illustrates one of the ways of approaching a session where incest is revealed.

Revealing Incest

Janice was referred to us from the hospital where she had been treated after a suicide attempt. She had two adolescent children from a first husband whom she had divorced. She had recently married a man who was the only child of a widowed mother.

Soon after the marriage, the husband's mother became very ill, and he began to spend time taking care of her and helping her financially. Janice thought she was being neglected while the husband spent so much time with his mother. He said it was his obligation and he couldn't do otherwise. She insisted and finally told him that he had to choose between his mother and her. He said that if she put it that way, he had to choose his mother, and they separated.

Janice became depressed to the point that she felt she couldn't take care of her children. She sent her son to live with her mother and sent her daughter, Hillary, to the other grandmother, the first husband's mother. With the children gone, Janice became even more depressed and attempted suicide. She was hospitalized.

While she was in the hospital, she learned that Hillary had also been hospitalized in a different place for a suicide attempt. Hillary told the doctors that she had attempted suicide because her father had tried to sexually molest her and had fondled her at her grandmother's house.

When Janice started therapy with Sandra Cohen at the Family Therapy Institute, she appeared depressed, immature, and very confused about her family relationships. She had a very bad relationship with her mother, yet she had given her own son to her. Her opinion of her first husband was very poor, yet she had given her daughter to his mother. Janice had such problems with self-esteem that she appeared to assume that anyone could be a better parent to her children.

Observing Janice from behind the one-way mirror, I thought that she must have had a traumatic childhood. I suggested to Sandra to ask her what was the worst thing that had happened to her in her life. Janice related how she had been sexually abused by her uncle during her whole adolescence. She talked about how she had wanted to protect Hillary from that kind of experience and had failed. Her mother had not protected her from the uncle. She even suspected that her mother knew about the incest. Sandra convinced her to invite the mother to a session to find out whether she had actually known. We couldn't invite the uncle because he was seriously ill in the hospital.

When Brenda, Janice's mother, came in, she sat far away from Janice, on an opposite couch. She was overweight, looked unhealthy, and moved with difficulty. Sandra said that she had wanted Brenda to come in to clarify some issues with her daughter, since Janice seemed uncertain about her mother's love.

"If I haven't shown her love all these years," said Brenda indignantly, "I must be doing something wrong. I have even told her. She has a wall around her—she put that wall around her a long time ago."

The wall that Brenda is referring to is the typical wall that the victim of incest builds around herself for fear of revealing the secret of incest to her mother. Brenda had noticed the distancing but didn't seem to know the reason.

"The reason I built a wall around me, Mom," said Janice, "is that from a very young age it was either put my wall up or get stepped on and hurt. You tried to teach me how to cook and I spilled something, and what did you tell me? I was clumsy and I couldn't do anything. I've had these little digs that stuck to me."

Janice's complaints are also typical of a victim of incest. Instead of addressing the important issue—the fact that her mother didn't protect her from sexual abuse—she complained bitterly about trivia.

"You remember these things," said Brenda, "that are different from what I remember. . . ."

Sandra interrupted, "I think this is a good time to pull down that wall you were talking about."

"But see, I don't remember it that way," said Brenda. "I tried to teach her to cook and she didn't want to measure anything. She wanted to do it her way."

"What I would like you to do now," said Sandra, "is for each of you to tell the other what is the worst thing that happened to you in your life."

"You mean the worst thing that happened between me and her?" asked Janice.

"Or the worst thing that happened to you in your life and you would like to tell her openly today," answered Sandra.

"The worst thing," said Janice, gesturing strongly with her whole arm moving up and down for emphasis, "was that I didn't feel I was being protected as a child. That's what I feel mostly upset about. OK? Mostly upset about that I got into a situation that I felt my mother as a mother should know that I shouldn't have gotten into. And there should have been protection."

"Do you want to talk about that?" asked Sandra.

"Well, I don't know if my mother knows 'cause we've never discussed this. I don't know if she knows about it. I don't know if I should just bring it up," said Janice, now gesturing with both arms. "I think she knows what I'm talking about. You don't let," she said turning to her mother, "a twenty-six-year-old man sleep in the same room with your daughter because there's no beds."

"What are you talking about?" asked Brenda frowning and in a shrill voice.

"See?" Janice made a gesture of hopelessness in Sandra's direction. "Uncle Jack being in the room with me, Mom! You don't remember that? You don't remember him sleeping in the same room with me because there were no beds?"

"No, I don't!" exclaimed the mother. "And if I had . . . I don't even remember it. . . . But he was your uncle!" she screamed. "But no, I don't even remember it, because you had your place upstairs. When? Where?"

"Mom, in Takoma Park, where we had the basement."

"No, I don't remember it."

"OK," said Janice, shaking her head hopelessly.

"I do not remember it," said Brenda emphatically. "And if I didn't protect you, I didn't know I didn't protect you. I thought I did."

"I would like you to explain to your mother exactly what happened," said Sandra. "I know that it's very difficult."

"I adored my uncle," said Janice, "because my father wasn't around. My father and I had a closeness to the point where I felt I couldn't do anything wrong, OK? But he wasn't around that much, so I adored my uncle. From a young age I remember him walking up to me and I ran up to him, and that was the kind of bond we had. All I remember vaguely is that there was no place for him to sleep so he slept in my room with me. And at that point I didn't mind 'cause I adored this man! I felt maybe he would treat me like I'm not stupid or I can't do anything! So we got into something physical and I didn't want to say no because I adored him!"

"What exactly happened?" asked Sandra.

"What do you mean 'exactly happened'? We made love!" Janice gestured with both arms raised as she had been doing throughout the session. "That was at thirteen!"

I called Sandra on the intercom suggesting she couldn't let that statement pass. It hadn't been "love"—it was rape. Part of the seduction by the offender is to confuse the victim as to what "love" is. In therapy that confusion must be clarified so there is no idealization of the incestuous or abusive relationship.

Janice turned to her mother. "When I was eleven, you let Uncle Jack and his friend Bob take me out to a gun range!"

"That's because I trusted him!" exclaimed Brenda. "I trusted him! It didn't dawn on me that he would do anything! If you trusted him, why shouldn't I have trusted him?" Brenda pointed at her chest. "He was my brother! He was your uncle, but he was also my brother! And I don't remember him even staying in the basement!"

"This was in Takoma Park," said Janice, "where we had the basement."

"That's what I'm saying," said Brenda. "I don't remember him even staying over. So I don't remember it! But all you had to do was come to me!"

"OK," said Janice looking at Sandra and gesturing with both hands for the mother to be quiet, "let me explain really quick before she gets more upset. Let me explain something. I would have if I felt someone was going to listen to me. I was thirteen and before that I was getting these mixed signals, and I figured that if I went to her she'd say 'I'm busy,' or 'That didn't really happen.' That's my perception, and to this point I didn't realize that she didn't know nothing about it."

Sandra turned to the mother. "I think you have to take responsibility for what happened to her when she was thirteen. She was only a child and she needed protection." The therapist made a mistake in the wording of this statement. She should have said, "I think that you should take responsibility for not having protected Janice from her uncle." By saying instead "for what happened to her," Sandra implies that Brenda should take responsibility for the sexual abuse itself, which is not appropriate.

"How can I take responsibility when I didn't even know what was going on? I thought I was protecting her the best way I could. I take responsibility for something I didn't know was happening?" asked Brenda, indignantly pointing at her chest while Janice made gestures to quiet her.

"Mom, how could you not have known he slept in my room?"

"Let me say something," said Sandra. "What happened was: a man, twenty-six years old, raped a thirteen-year-old girl."

Brenda interrupted angrily, "I know what you're saying, but I tell you I didn't know it!"

"I know you didn't know it," interrupted Sandra.

"How can I be blamed for something? I thought I was protecting her the best way I could!" continued Brenda. "And now you're telling me I was an unfit mother?"

What has been most important in this interchange is what Brenda has not said. She has just discovered that her daughter was sexually molested at age thirteen, and she has not yet shown any compassion or concern for Janice, only indignation and anger. What people don't say to each other is often more important than what they do say. It's the absence of the warm gesture that defines the coldness of the relationship.

"No!" asserted Janice, emphatically. "We're not saying that, Mom!"

"Let me clarify one thing," said Sandra. "I'm not blaming you for what happened. The blame goes directly to your brother. He was the one who raped her. What I'm asking you is to take responsibility for the things that you didn't do as a mother in the past. The mistakes that you made. Not having enough good communication with your daughter that she would have come to you and told you what happened. Not seeing the signs that this was going on for three years. For allowing a man, and I know you don't remember, but this happened . . . for allowing a twenty-six-year-old man to sleep in her bedroom."

"He did not sleep in her bedroom," interrupted Brenda emphatically. "I don't care what she says!"

"See what I mean?" interrupted Janice, addressing Sandra with her arms open in a gesture of despair.

"Alright, I will take responsibility," continued Brenda. "I was wrong; I didn't protect her. I didn't see the signs. I knew this was exactly what was going to happen. I knew I was going to be the villain. It was all my fault. That's it. Alright. I take responsibility for allowing him to sleep with her although I don't remember doing it."

"Maybe you should ask him," said Janice. "He'll tell you the truth."

"Yes, I intend to," said Brenda.

"Do you think I'm lying?" asked Janice pointing to her chest indignantly.

"No," said Brenda pointing her finger at Janice, "I didn't say that, and I don't mean asking him—I mean telling him!"

"Let me say something," said Sandra. "When sexual abuse happens, it's very painful for the victim. It's a pain that is not just physical and emotional—it's a spiritual pain."

"I know that. I went through that myself," said Brenda. "I know exactly what you're talking about."

"You lived through that yourself?" asked Sandra.

"Yes, I did."

"OK," said Sandra. She was surprised at the mother's quick understanding of the spiritual pain. Sandra had been very reluctant to invite Brenda to this session. She felt that no good would come from it and it would just be an unpleasant confrontation. Also, at this point, she had had no experience in working with sexual abuse or in talking about spiritual pain (now she is one of our best therapists of sex offenders and their victims).

"Only I was just five," continued Brenda.

"Have you talked with Janice about that?"

"No, it's nobody's business but my own. And that was my grandfather! And I was only five years old! And I was also raped when I was sixteen. I know what turmoil it is. That's why I tried to do the best I could for her. If I'd known, it wouldn't have happened. But you're telling me I didn't protect her. I tried my best. My best was not good enough, but I didn't know that."

"That's why," said Sandra, "you need to take responsibility for your best not being good enough at that point. What I would like you to do now is to tell Janice that you are really sorry that you couldn't protect her at the time, that you weren't able to see the signs. Because you know the pain she has because you have the same pain inside, and she needs to hear that you're really sorry that you couldn't protect her."

Brenda turned to Janice and exclaimed with sincerity, "I am

sorry!" (Janice nodded her head affirmatively.) "I'm very sorry I didn't protect you, but I couldn't protect something I didn't know was going on. I'm sorry that you got mixed signals. I did the best I could. I was working. . . ."

"I understand," interrupted Janice, "because I've done the same thing with my kids."

"What you don't understand," continued Brenda, "is that I was so afraid I was going to lose my job because I had to work overtime on my own without getting paid for it, to get my work done because of the extreme headaches which no one knew. I could have had the tumor all my life."

Brenda continued explaining that at the time when Janice was abused, she was suffering from such intense headaches that she couldn't finish her work within office hours. Years later it was discovered that she had a brain tumor and it was removed, but at the time she had been a single mother struggling to support her children while coping with extreme chronic pain. My plan had been to insist that Sandra get the mother on her knees to apologize for not having protected Janice from her uncle, but, hearing about the brain tumor, I thought this would be too much to ask for in one session.

"I was trying to make myself indispensable," continued Brenda. "It took three hours every day at night to get my work done so I would have a job to support you and your brother." Brenda's voice was cracking with stress, and she was tearful.

"Something that should not happen again in the family," said Sandra, "is secrecy. Because secrets are the element for this to continue into the next generation, and you want this to stop right now."

"Yes," said Janice, "the hard thing as a kid is when you're not sure that anyone is going to believe you."

"That's why your job as a mother now is to protect your daughter so that nobody hurts her and to teach her to talk about these things. I want the two of you to promise each other that this is not going to happen in the next generation."

"What's not going to happen?" asked Janice. "The secret, the abuse?"

"The abuse and the secret," said Sandra. "The two of you have to make sure that it doesn't happen again. It happened to you," said Sandra to Brenda, "it happened to your daughter; it happened to your grandchild; it might have happened in previous generations. It has to stop now."

"The only thing you can do," said Janice, "is try to be observant, watch what's going on and not close your eyes."

Sandra turned to the mother. "I would like you to tell your daughter that she's the best mother and protector for Hillary, that no one but Janice will love her the way she loves her." Sandra looked at Janice. "Because you sent her to live with another family because of your low self-esteem, because you don't believe in your-self, but there's no reason for you to feel like that. You love her with all your soul. And I would like you, Brenda, to tell her that she's the best mother for Hillary."

Brenda turned to Janice. "I've been telling you all this time that you're the best mother for Hillary!"

"I would like to invite you to come the next week," said Sandra to Brenda.

"No," said Janice, "no, because all we're going to do is sit here and have this backlash again. No, it's never going to change. The only thing I wanted to get straight across is what I felt, thinking all this time that she knew, that was all."

"Janice does not want a relationship with me," said Brenda, "you can see it right now. I don't think she'll ever have a relationship with me until she can get rid of a lot of things in her own head, until she can resolve things, until she can stop blaming me for a lot of things in the past. Until she makes peace with herself, she'll never be able to make peace with me."

"It's not just in the past," said Janice. "I don't like the way she is right now. I don't like the way she's treating my son, and that's why I can't talk to her. When I go around my son, I'm a third wheel, OK? And that's why I cannot be around her. I cannot be around her because I'll say something, she'll say something, and we'll be like this." Janice gestured pulling her arms apart to signal a great separation.

The session ended on this sour note. Sandra insisted that at some point she would like to see the mother again and help them with their relationship, but she made an appointment to see Janice alone the next week.

When Sandra came to talk with me behind the one-way mirror, she said, "See, I told you it would be unpleasant and not turn out well."

"Just wait," I said, "it takes a while for relationships to change. Give them time."

The next week, Janice called a few minutes before her next appointment and asked whether the time could be changed to later in the afternoon. Sandra agreed. Janice came in looking very pretty and cheerful and told Sandra that she had called to change the appointment because she had run into her mother and her son at the market and Brenda had invited her to lunch.

"She came up to me at the store," said Janice, "and I said 'Hello.' I said 'Hi' to my son. She came up and gave me a hug; I gave her a hug back. She told me she loved me. I told her I loved her. I said, 'Let's just forget it and let's just go on.'"

"Wow!" said Sandra. "I'm really glad!"

"It was nice," said Janice. She was smiling from ear to ear.

"That's wonderful!"

"It was nice. So then when she said lunch, I said, 'Let me call.' I didn't think you would mind too much."

"No, that was wonderful. I'm really happy that you had lunch with your mother."

"It was nice. It was a very eventful day because we went to an Italian restaurant. We sat there. We talked. My son asked me a question that threw me off guard." She laughed. "He asked me why I fell in love with my husband. He said, 'Is it alright to ask? I don't want to pry.' And I said, 'No, you have the right to ask.' And I told him."

"He must have felt very good about you to be able to ask that question," said Sandra.

Janice nodded agreement. "It was good. It was the first time that we were all able to sit together and enjoy. What happened when she was here was that I realized that we basically had the same feelings." She gestured with her hands putting them together. "So that instead of my being the little girl with her over me, I realized I had to take care of some of those little-girl feelings and those little-girl attitudes. Now, no matter what I do, she is still my mother. . . ."

"And she loves you," interrupted Sandra.

"She does love me. And we may not totally agree, but she is still my mother. Since we came to see you, there's like a big cloud lifted off of me—a big burden. I mean, I can say, 'I was molested by him. OK.' There is no little-girl hurt feeling to the pit of my stomach any more. I can almost stand back and say, 'This happened,' and I can still go on. It's not going to take my life. There's something else I want to tell you, and I know we don't have much time, but one thing you brought up is communicating with my family. When I did that I realized how much I love them and care for them, but that also puts me back to how much I love and I miss my husband. So I did something last week." She shook her head mischievously.

"What did you do?" asked Sandra.

"I called him up," Janice sighed.

"How was it?" asked Sandra.

"Well, I was a little nervous," said Janice giggling nervously. "I called him early in the morning. I said, 'Look, I know you have to work. Don't get mad. I didn't mean to call you this early in the morning, but I had to talk to you. You haven't called. I don't know what's going on, and I just was curious about what's going on.' He said, 'No problem, it's no problem.'" She giggled like a teenager. "We talked for a while and I said, 'We can't talk too long, you've got to get to work.' He said, 'Well, can I see you later?' I said, 'You don't have to do that. I just wanted to see what was going on.' And he said, 'I really want to see you later.' So I said, 'OK.' He came over that night and we sat there and talked. I said . . . I put it very point-blank: 'I don't want you coming over here and we ending up into something else.' I said, 'If you come over, I want to talk. I think we really need to talk.' So he did, and we sat there for three hours and talked."

After that conversation, Janice and her husband reconciled and Hillary came back to live with them. The relationship between Janice and Brenda continued to be warm and friendly. Now that Janice had her mother, she could allow her husband to have his.

•   •   •   •   •   •   •

Probably the most important principle of my approach to the therapy of violence is the redistribution of responsibility and shame. Typically, it's the victim who feels responsible and carries the shame. The first step toward relieving her of this burden is to relieve her of the secret that she has carried, perhaps for years. It is never too late. Relationships can change, and even those who have been estranged for a long time can share the joy of reconciliation.

Epilogue

Given the current epidemic of violence in our society, the reader probably still has many unanswered questions about violence in the family and about a therapy of social action. I will try to imagine some of these questions and answer them.

How Much of Violence Can Actually Be Treated in Therapy? The answer is all kinds. If we cannot solve a problem of violence in therapy, it's not because people can't change; it's because as therapists we are not intelligent or knowledgeable enough to bring about change. In fact, a therapy of social action is based on the belief that people can change themselves and stop their own violence.

Everyone has the potential to change if they want to change. There is always a choice to be made. Even the worst psychopath, sadistic batterer, homicidal husband, or compulsive pedophile can change if they so desire. The problem for therapists is that sometimes these people come to therapy because they are court-ordered but not because they feel any remorse or have any wish to change. The goal is then to motivate them so they will want to be different, so they can envision another self, another life, a better future. We all have the potential to lead many possible different lives. The art of the therapist is to make a different life possible.

The therapist of social action is always optimistic but never gullible. We can always offer therapy, even to those who are serving life sentences in jail, and we can always offer the possibility of a better life, even in jail. But that doesn't mean that we would recommend the reintegration in society of certain criminals. Sometimes the risk is too great. The state of the art of therapy is such that we can promise a high probability of good results, but we cannot give assurance that any one particular individual will not reoffend.

HOW MUCH OF VIOLENCE CAN BE ATTRIBUTED TO ANGER? The question is irrelevant. We cannot use feelings to justify actions. Anger does not lead inevitably to violence and is therefore not an excuse. In a therapy of social action, we hold each person responsible for his or her emotions.

HOW MUCH OF VIOLENCE CAN BE ATTRIBUTED TO FRUSTRATION AND DISPLACEMENT GENERATED BY RACISM OR ECONOMIC HARDSHIP? Social injustice doesn't necessarily lead to violence, particularly against one's own family. A therapist of social action believes that people have some inalienable human rights: the right to shelter, sustenance, medical treatment, education, and protection from violence. Yet the violation of these human rights does not justify violence. We always have a choice.

The counterparts of human rights are human obligations. As human beings we have the obligation to ensure that everyone on the planet benefits from the right to shelter, sustenance, medical treatment, education, and protection from violence. Not to act to ensure these rights, to remain neutral, is to be on the side of abuse and violence. Therapists in particular must protect these rights because they have so much power to do good or harm.

· · · · · · ·

The following are some aphorisms that I think are particularly useful to help therapists stay on track while working with problems of violence. They were inspired by the aphorisms of Baltasar Gracian.

KNOW HOW TO READ MINDS. Be sensitive to truths that are half-spoken. Know how to take a hint. This is at the basis of the intelligence of the therapist. Learn how to guess accurately people's emotions and intentions.

FIND EACH PERSON'S "HANDLE." The art of moving people consists of knowing how to motivate them. You must get inside each person to understand what they want, what they enjoy, their dreams and desires. The trick is to find what sets people in motion.

BE SINCERE AND TRUTHFUL. To be deceitful with your clients is to betray them. It is better to be trustworthy than clever. Be always on the side of the truth.

BE KIND. It helps to win people over. As a therapist, you can do a great deal of good. The good that you do will be best appreciated if it comes from someone with a kindly manner.

THINK CAREFULLY ABOUT WHAT IS MOST IMPORTANT. Therapists fail by not conceptualizing what is happening. They miss their opportunities because they don't perceive them. They don't understand when they are doing more harm than good. Some are confused and focus their attention on what is unimportant, ignoring that which truly matters. The wise therapist is not afraid to decide what is important.

KNOW HOW TO USE METAPHOR AND INSINUATION. This is the greatest subtlety of interaction. Metaphor and insinuation can be used to give powerful suggestions and to discover truths. If the therapist is careless, this power can be destructive. You must know not only how to communicate in metaphor and how to insinuate but also how to understand the metaphors and insinuations of others.

QUIT WHILE YOU'RE AHEAD. You must know when to end a session, when to stop using an intervention, when to end a therapy. Each session must have closure. It must end with suspense or when something has been accomplished, like a scene in a play. Don't undo your good work by overdoing it.

KNOW WHEN THE MOMENT IS RIPE, AND KNOW HOW TO TAKE ADVANTAGE OF IT. It is easiest to influence people when they are in a crisis, when they are upset, when they are asking for help. Don't miss the moment. Engage with them immediately, and intervene quickly. People are more amenable to influence at the beginning of therapy than during the course of it.

NEVER EXAGGERATE. To use superlatives is the language of the weak. It casts doubts on your intelligence and reveals a lack of knowledge. Exaggeration is particularly harmful when it raises expectations that lead to disappointment. Exaggerating pain and evil is the most harmful of all since it leads to hopelessness. Show restraint in your communication. Exaggeration is a form of lying.

AVOID DISAGREEMENTS. Avoid both being contradicted and contradicting others in therapy. Keep your thoughts and your feelings to yourself, and speak only when you have prepared others to accept what you say. Dissent is often taken as insult and makes it impossible to discover the truth and to do therapy.

BE SUSPICIOUS, BUT CONCEAL YOUR SUSPICIONS. As a therapist you must be always suspicious, never totally believing anyone. But do not reveal your suspicions so as not to lose the confidence of others. Because suspiciousness offends, make every effort to appear thoughtful and concerned rather than suspicious.

CONTROL YOUR DISLIKES. We feel aversion toward some people even before we get to know them. Keep this tendency in check. There is nothing more antitherapeutic than to dislike those one needs to help. What a therapist needs to feel is appreciation, not contempt.

AVOID DANGEROUS SITUATIONS. Don't take risks when there is the possibility of violence, whether self-inflicted or against others. Do the work of therapy only after you have taken all precautions against violence. Be careful not to place others in danger.

KNOW HOW TO CHOOSE. There are endless possibilities of what to say and do in therapy, but you must choose and choose the best. Many intelligent therapists are lost when they have to choose between alternatives. They can't decide on the one best course of action and end up doing a little of this, some of that, and accomplishing nothing. Wisdom is knowing how to choose.

Be Quick to Carry Out What You Have Slowly and Carefully Planned. Therapy must be planned, and the planning takes place outside of the therapy session. Think cautiously, but speak and act without hesitation. Be ready to grasp the right moment to put your plans into action. Do not postpone an intervention unnecessarily. Many therapists go wrong out of neglect.

Be Patient. Patience is kindness. Feel comfortable with the passing of time until you find your opportunity. The timing of an intervention is crucial to its success. People vary in the timing of their communication and their reactions. Pace yourself to the timing of those you wish to influence.

Remind People About the Future. Many people fail to do good things because it never occurs to them. Point them in the right direction. It is a great gift to be able to evaluate one's possibilities. Otherwise, many successes never take place. The therapist, skilled at projecting into the future and at evaluating alternatives, must give this skill to others, sometimes directly, sometimes merely dropping hints. Remember that most of the time, things are not obtained because they were not attempted.

Therapy Is the Art of Preparation. Never give a directive or make a suggestion if you know it will fail. It would be foolish to do so. It is better to wait, ask, converse until you have done sufficient preparations that you know you will succeed.

Don't Take Things Too Seriously. Know when not to make too much of something. Some problems are solved if left alone. Others become serious because we pay attention to them. Sometimes the therapy causes the problem. Know what not to bother with and when to leave good enough alone.

See the Good in Everything and Everyone. Emphasize the positive. Everything and everyone has something good. Focus on the strengths. Focusing on defects leads to bitterness and sorrow.

Don't Be Paradoxical Because You Want to Be Original. Paradox is deceitful and threatens the dignity of others if it is designed to satisfy the therapist. Paradox possesses a false charm that can lead to the wrong outcome. It is wrong to use paradox only because a therapist cannot be straightforward and kind.

AGREE WITH OTHERS SO THAT THEY WILL AGREE WITH YOU. This is a strategy for getting people to follow your suggestions. The more frequently you say yes, the easier it will be for others to say yes instead of no to you. In this way, you overcome resistance.

BE SKILLFUL IN CONVERSATION. It is the therapist's only instrument. The art of conversation is the measure of excellence of therapy. Every word that is said counts. Every statement is therapeutic or antitherapeutic. You must know what you want to say, then say precisely that, and say it in such a way that you adjust your language to the language of others.

BE SKILLFUL AT MASTERING YOUR ANGER. The first thing to do when you are upset is to notice that you are. The second is to decide not to let your emotions go any further. If you are careful to do this, you can quickly end your anger and gain self-control. Know how to stop and do it at the right moment. Anger detracts from reason and compassion, the two most important qualities in a therapist.

DON'T HOLD TOO FIRMLY TO ANY PLAN. It is foolish to be stubborn. Be ready to make concessions. Don't continue to do what is failing. If a plan doesn't work, change it.

KNOW HOW TO PRAISE, AND ALWAYS FIND SOMETHING TO PRAISE. It sets the right tone and is a good subject of conversation. Make praise a habit instead of looking for things to criticize.

BE PEACEABLE. Convey that you are at peace with yourself, that you believe in "to live and let live." Show that you can listen and see, but keep quiet. Inspire others to be at peace.

PROVIDE SOMETHING TO HOPE FOR. Everyone needs something to look forward to. The spirit is always yearning for things; curiosity needs something to feed on. Hope keeps us alive. Arrange for everyone in therapy to have something to look forward to in the future, be it in a month or in a year or more. Help people discover what they want. When people want nothing, you should fear for them.

LISTEN TO WHAT PEOPLE SAY BUT PAY ATTENTION TO WHAT THEY DO. Therapy is an exchange of words that leads to a change of actions. Therapy is only therapeutic when it is action oriented. You must change not only how people express themselves but also what they do with their lives.

KNOW HOW TO FORGET AND HELP OTHERS DO THE SAME. The things that should most be forgotten are often the ones most easily remembered. Not only do we often fail to remember the positive, but often we remember the negative precisely when we shouldn't. Memory can give us pain and prevent happiness. Sometimes the best remedy for troubles is to forget them. The memory must be trained to remember what we truly want to remember.

＊ ＊ ＊ ＊ ＊ ＊ ＊

I hope that this book has brought some hope to therapists working with violence in the family. To hurt those whom we love is the greatest pain of all. It is the worst horror in the world of humans. I hope this book has helped a little in creating a reality that struggles against that horror.

Notes

Introduction

The story of Pandora was told by Virginia Hamilton in *In the Beginning: Creation Stories from Around the World* (New York: Harcourt Brace Jovanovich, 1988).

Chapter Five

Maya Angelou talks about her childhood in *I Know Why the Caged Bird Sings* (New York: Bantam, 1971).

The quotes from Thich Nhat Hanh and Rabbi Shelomo are from Molly Young Brown (ed.), *Lighting a Candle: Quotations on the Spiritual Life* (New York: HarperCollins, 1994).

Hanna Arendt discusses the banality of evil in *Eichmann in Jerusalem* (New York: Viking Penguin, 1977).

Chapter Six

A transcript of excerpts of the therapy of a juvenile sex offender and his family can be found in my book *Sex, Love and Violence* (New York: W.W.Norton, 1990).

Chapter Seven

For more on negotiating in marriage, see James P. Keim, "Triangulation and the Art of Negotiation." in the *Journal of Systemic Therapies*, (Ontario, Canada, Winter, 1993, pp.76–87).

Epilogue

The aphorisms that inspired me can be found in Baltasar Gracian, *The Art of Worldly Wisdom* (New York: Doubleday, 1992).

Index

S

About the Author

· ·

CLOÉ MADANES is one of the world's most respected authorities on marital and family relationships and on the process of change in families. She directs the Family Therapy Institute of Washington, D.C., located in Rockville, Maryland, and is a distinguished lecturer, consultant, and workshop leader. Her books, *Strategic Family Therapy, Behind the One-Way Mirror, Sex, Love and Violence,* and *The Secret Meaning of Money,* have won international acclaim and have been published in more than six languages.

Communications to the author or requests for information about her seminars should be addressed to the Family Therapy Institute, 5850 Hubbard Drive, Rockville, Maryland 20852.